ANNUAL UPDATE

US GOVERNMENT & POLITICS

Anthony J. Bennett

HODDER
EDUCATION
AN HACHETTE UK COMPANY

Hodder Education, an Hachette UK company, Blenheim Court, George Street, Banbury, Oxfordshire OX16 5BH

Orders

Bookpoint Ltd, 130 Park Drive, Milton Park, Abingdon, Oxfordshire OX14 4SE
tel: 01235 827720
fax: 01235 400401
e-mail: education@bookpoint.co.uk

Lines are open 9.00 a.m.–5.00 p.m., Monday to Saturday, with a 24-hour message answering service. You can also order through the Hodder Education website: www.hoddereducation.co.uk

© Anthony J. Bennett 2018

ISBN 978-1-5104-1639-0

First printed 2018
Impression number 5 4 3 2 1
Year 2021 2020 2019 2018

Typeset by Integra Software Services Pvt. Ltd., Pondicherry, India

Printed by CPI Group (UK) Ltd, Croydon, CR0 4YY

Hachette UK's policy is to use papers that are natural, renewable and recyclable products and made from wood grown in sustainable forests. The logging and manufacturing processes are expected to conform to the environmental regulations of the country of origin.

Contents

Chapter 1 Checks and balances in the era of Donald Trump   1

The Founders' fears and provisions ■ Checks by the courts ■ Checks by
Congress

Chapter 2 To what extent can a president reshape the Supreme Court?   9

Why so important? ■ Reshaping the Court in practice ■ Conclusion

Chapter 3 The Supreme Court: the 2016–17 term   15

The Court and the separation of church and state ■ The death penalty
■ Overview of the 2016–17 term ■ And the future?

Chapter 4 Grand juries, special prosecutors, pardons and impeachment   23

Grand jury ■ Special prosecutor ■ Presidential pardons ■ Impeachment

Chapter 5 More from the 2016 elections   29

The popular vote ■ Third-party votes ■ Electoral College votes
■ Split districts ■ Senate races

Chapter 6 The 2018 midterm congressional elections   36

Alabama's special Senate election ■ Senate elections ■ House elections

Chapter 7 Where is the Democratic Party going?   43

Down, down, down ■ Down and divided ■ The Democrats' white
working-class problem ■ Likely positives for Democrats in 2018…
■ …and likely negatives ■ A Better Deal? ■ And what about
2020? ■ Two health warnings

Chapter 8 Is the Trump cabinet merely a mirror image of the president?   52

A reflection of the boss ■ Recruiting elected politicians ■ Gender
■ Race ■ Age ■ The cabinet as a mirror of Trump ■ Senate
confirmation ■ Other cabinet members ■ Replacement appointments
■ Cabinet meetings

Contents

Chapter 9 The Trump presidency: an early assessment   62

Trump is trying to govern as the outsider he promised to be ■ Trump
has little interest in legislation ■ Trump's White House has been largely
dysfunctional ■ The Trump administration is dogged by scandal
and apparent dishonesty ■ Trump's approval ratings have been at
historically low levels ■ Donald Trump is a deeply polarising figure

Who's who in US politics 2018   73

Checks and balances in the era of Donald Trump

What you need to know

- The Founding Fathers based the Constitution on a series of checks and balances between the three branches of the federal government — Congress, the president and the courts.
- They were especially careful to check the power of the president to safeguard the nation against tyranny by the executive branch.
- Congress's main checks on the executive branch include: the power to amend, block or reject the president's legislative proposals; the power to investigate the actions of executive branch officials, including the president; and the power to confirm appointments to the executive and judiciary (Senate only).

The Founders' fears and provisions

Writing in the tenth essay of *The Federalist Papers* in the autumn of 1787, James Madison warned that 'enlightened statesmen will not always be at the helm' of the nation. He continued:

> Men of factious tempers, of local prejudices, or of sinister designs, may, by intrigue, by corruption, or by other means, first obtain the suffrages, and then betray the interests, of the people.

Madison was right. But even Madison could never have foreseen Donald Trump. Writing a few months later in 1788, Madison had more to say on the way the chief executive of the newly proposed Republic should be hedged around with checks and balances to avoid the possibility of executive tyranny:

> Ambition must be made to counteract ambition. The interest of the man must be connected with the constitutional rights of the place. If men were angels, no government would be necessary. If angels were to govern men, neither external nor internal controls on government would be necessary.

So the Constitution was to act as a safeguard for 'the defect of better motives' (see Box 1.1) by relying on 'opposite and rival interests' — what we know as the Constitution's checks and balances.

The 44 men — and they are all men — who have filled the office of the presidency since 1789 have been a varied bunch. There have been those who have generally appealed to the nation's highest aspirations — George Washington, Abraham Lincoln, Franklin Roosevelt and Ronald Reagan. Their policies and motives may not have been flawless, but they reflected the 'better angels' rather than the devilishness of humankind. But there have been characteristics among that 44 from which the Founders wisely wanted to protect the nation — Andrew Jackson's rage, Millard Fillmore's bigotry, James Buchanan's incompetence, Theodore Roosevelt's self-aggrandisement, Warren Harding's corruption and Richard Nixon's paranoia.

A regular topic of debate in American politics is the extent to which the checks and balances — especially those specifically designed by the Founding Fathers well over 200 years ago — still work today. Are these constitutional checks, devised in the eighteenth century, adaptable to the government and politics of the twenty-first century? Of particular topical interest is whether the checks placed on the president can work as well in the era of Donald Trump as they did in the eras of, for example, George Washington (1789–97) or Woodrow Wilson (1913–21).

Checks by the courts

The Trump presidency was just 9 days old when the President received his first rebuff from the federal courts. This concerned Trump's so-called 'Muslim travel ban'. This all began back in December 2015 as the race for the Republican presidential nomination was just a few weeks away from the first primaries and caucuses. On 2 December, two people — both of Pakistani descent, but both lawfully present in the United States — opened fire in San Bernardino, California, killing 14 people and seriously injuring another 22. The two perpetrators had been radicalised online by Islamic terrorist groups based in Saudi Arabia. Immediately after this horrific incident, Mr Trump — then leading the polls in the Republican nomination contest — issued a statement that read:

Donald J. Trump is calling for a total and complete shutdown of Muslims entering the United States until our country's representatives can figure out what is going on.

The 'Muslim travel ban', as it became known, featured regularly in Trump's campaign speeches during the next year, and his core supporters saw its delivery as a litmus test of Trump's authenticity as the president who was going to 'make America great again'.

Exactly a week into his presidency, Trump issued Executive Order 13769 which banned the entry of people from seven Muslim-majority countries – Iran, Iraq, Libya, Somalia, Sudan, Syria and Yemen – for at least 90 days, regardless of whether or not they held valid visas. In the text of the order, the President justified the move by making a number of references to the 9/11 attacks on America in 2001. But none of the 9/11 terrorists came from any of these seven countries. Furthermore, noticeably missing from the list was Saudi Arabia – visited by the San Bernardino terrorists, and where Mr Trump has significant business interests. The result of the order was chaos at America's main entry points, most notably the country's largest airports.

In just 3 days, some 50 cases were filed in federal courts around the country calling on the courts to halt the order's implementation. On 29 January, within 48 hours of the order having been issued, a federal judge signed a temporary restraining order halting its implementation pending a more detailed court hearing. The following day, Acting Attorney General Sally Yates – a holdover from the Obama administration pending Senate confirmation of Trump's nominee – issued a statement barring any employee of the US Department of Justice from defending the President's order in court. Yates was immediately fired by the President.

By this time the state of Washington had filed a legal challenge to the Executive Order in federal court. On 3 February, in his decision in *State of Washington* v *Trump*, Judge James Robart ruled in favour of the state – and against the President – saying that the plaintiffs had 'demonstrated immediate and irreparable injury', extending the ban on Trump's order nationwide. The order foundered in court on account of it being found to be discriminatory on the basis of religion. Trump vented his anger on Twitter, describing Judge Robart as 'this so-called judge' and his decision as 'ridiculous' (see Box 1.2).

| Box 1.2 | President Trump on Twitter, 4 February 2017 |

- 'The opinion of this so-called judge, which essentially takes law-enforcement away from our country, is ridiculous and will be overturned.'
- 'What is our country coming to when a judge can halt a Homeland Security travel ban and anyone, even with bad intentions, can come into US?'
- 'Because the ban was lifted by a judge, many very bad and dangerous people may be pouring into our country. A terrible decision.'

That day, the cable television shows and the Twittersphere were awash with discussion as to whether, given his reaction on Twitter, the President might defy the court ruling. Not that Trump would have been the first president to go against a court order; examples can be found from the presidencies of both Abraham Lincoln and Franklin Roosevelt. But Trump did what Nixon did when the courts told him to hand over the incriminating White House tapes — he complied. We don't know why he just went along with it, but as Jack Goldsmith ('Will Donald Trump Destroy the Presidency?', *The Atlantic*, October 2017) commented: 'the most powerful man in the world complied with the edict of a little-known federal trial judge on an issue at the top of his agenda. The Constitution held.'

In March, the President signed a new Executive Order (13780), removing Iraq from the list of countries to which it applied. Three days later, this new order was itself the subject of a legal challenge when five states — Washington, Oregon, Hawaii, Massachusetts and Minnesota — filed a challenge in federal court. On 15 March, a federal judge in Hawaii, Derek Watson, issued a temporary restraining order that blocked the new order nationwide, a decision the President described as an 'unprecedented judicial overreach'. He even criticised his own second Executive Order — drawn up by his own Department of Justice — calling it a 'watered down version' of his first order. In its defence of the order in federal court, Department of Justice lawyers claimed that the order had nothing to do with religion, and everything to do with national security. The trouble was that in their judgements, the judges were quoting Candidate Trump's own words calling for a 'total and complete shutdown of Muslims entering the United States'. The President was hoisted by his own petard. Trump announced that he would challenge this latest decision in the federal appeal court. But when that challenge came to court in May, the appeal court upheld the blocking of Trump's second 'travel ban', prompting another Twitterstorm from the President, much of it directed against his own administration for not sticking with the first order. Though as the courts had also blocked that, the logic of the argument was unclear.

Finally, the whole thing made its way to the US Supreme Court where, on 26 June, the nine justices agreed to review the lower court decisions about Trump's second order suggesting that the lower court decisions were too broad and failed to give sufficient weight to the national security issues the president claimed to be addressing. However, in late September, the Supreme Court postponed that review after Trump issued yet another order seemingly even broader than the second. At time of going to press, this story was therefore still ongoing.

So what does all this tell us about the effectiveness of judicial checks on the presidency in the Trump era? Certainly the courts have shown a willingness to challenge the President even on issues at the very top of his political agenda when they believe that he has acted unconstitutionally. But have the courts acted properly? By that I mean, have they acted in the spirit of judicial neutrality and political impartiality? True, they were in a difficult position, but both the federal trial and appeal courts seemed at times to react with what Jack Goldsmith would later describe as 'hasty and in some ways sloppy judicial opinions'. In extending constitutional protection to non-citizens, indeed to those who lacked any connection at all with the United States, they left themselves open to the charge of offering opinion that was unsupported by any solid legal argument. In contrast, the Supreme Court offered a more 'sober, respectful and low-temperature opinion' that sent a strong signal about the importance of judicial impartiality even in — maybe especially in — such an era as this.

Checks by Congress

Conventional wisdom says that the checks by Congress on the president operate more effectively when the two institutions — the House of Representatives and the Senate — are controlled by different parties. It is thought that if the president's own party is in control of Congress, the two institutions will tend to operate more as lapdogs than watchdogs. But that has not been true of the Republican-controlled Congress during President Trump's first year.

The Republican-controlled Senate began by putting Trump's cabinet picks through their paces with unusual severity (see Chapter 8). When two Republican senators voted against Betsy DeVos as Trump's nominee for secretary of education, the Vice President was needed to break a tied vote and get her confirmed. This was the closest the Senate had come to rejecting a cabinet nominee in nearly 30 years. In mid-February, Senate scrutiny led Trump's nominee for secretary of labor, Andrew Puzder, to withdraw from the confirmation process fearing that he could not muster the necessary level of support even among Republicans.

Then at the start of March, the House Intelligence Committee opened an inquiry into allegations of Russian interference in the 2016 elections, something that the President had dismissed as 'fake news'. Both houses of Congress would continue to exercise their investigative checks on the President, and more widely on the executive branch, especially on matters relating to Trump's firing of FBI Director Comey (see Chapter 9).

In terms of legislation, Trump found the Republican-controlled Congress a significant check on his power no more so than in his flagship proposal to repeal and replace Obamacare. During the campaign in 2016, Trump had made oft-repeated promises to achieve this — and quickly.

- '**On my first day**, I am going to ask Congress to **immediately** send me a bill to repeal and replace Obamacare.' (September 2016)
- 'You're going to have such great health care at a tiny fraction of the cost. And it's **going to be so easy**.' (October)
- 'When we win on November 8 and elect a Republican Congress, we will be able to **immediately** repeal and replace Obamacare.' (November)

'On my first day', 'immediately' and 'it's going to be so easy.' Hardly surprising that Trump's core supporters were expecting action — and fast. And as Trump prepared to take office during the transition, he was still ramping up the expectations:

- 'It will be repeal and replace. It will be essentially simultaneously.' (January 2017)

But once in office, Trump quickly began to sing a different tune. 'Nobody knew that health care could be so complicated,' the President claimed within his first month in office. Nobody?

President Obama had spent the best part of his first 14 months in office working for legislation on healthcare reform. There were numerous meetings at the White House, visits to Capitol Hill, meetings with interest groups on both sides of the argument, plus a daunting series of town hall meetings round the country. By contrast, President Trump gave the appearance that healthcare reform would just drop into his lap — or onto his desk — at a whistle or a tweet. True, the Republicans in Congress had spent the best part of the last 6 years passing legislation to repeal Obamacare — but without ever saying in detail what they would put in its place. That, of course, was the tricky part.

But Congress — even a Republican Congress — was not about to be rolled over by the President. Even many Republicans were sceptical about the alternatives to Obamacare that their own leadership was supporting. All the Democrats were implacably opposed to removing President Obama's flagship legislative achievement. But with comparatively small majorities in both chambers, the Republicans had to keep most of their own members onside if they were to achieve anything.

Things began in the House in late March with a damp squib as a much-promised vote to repeal and replace Obamacare was first postponed (23 March) and then delayed indefinitely (24 March) due to what House Speaker Paul Ryan admitted was simply lack of support. On 27 April another attempt to pass healthcare reform in the House had to be aborted. They had hoped to pass something before Trump's first 100 days were up — on the 29th — but to no avail. However a week later, the House voted 217–213 to repeal and replace Obamacare. All 217 'yes' votes were cast by Republicans while all 193 Democrats, joined by 20 Republicans, voted 'no'. Nine of the 20 Republicans who voted 'no' were what we shall call in Chapter 5 'Clinton Republicans' — that is Republican members of the House whose districts voted for Democrat Hillary Clinton in 2016. As Table 1.1 shows, it was hardly surprising that Republicans like Ileana Ros-Lehtinen, Barbara Comstock and Mike Coffman joined House Democrats in voting 'no' on the American Health Care Act as they all come from districts in which Hillary Clinton beat Donald Trump by a sizeable margin in 2016.

Table 1.1 Selected 'Clinton Republicans' in the House who voted 'no' on the American Health Care Act, 4 May 2017

House member	District	Trump's vote in their district in 2016 (%)	Clinton's vote in their district in 2016 (%)
Ileana Ros-Lehtinen	Florida 27	38.9	58.5
Barbara Comstock	Virginia 10	42.2	52.2
Mike Coffman	Colorado 6	41.3	50.2

Delay followed delay in the Senate as a number of Republicans opposed the repeal and replace legislation. The most ardent critics were Lisa Murkowski of Alaska and Susan Collins of Maine, but by mid-July they had been joined by Mike Lee of Utah and Jerry Moran of Kansas. The Republican leadership in the Senate — with only 52 votes at their disposal — could afford to lose only two votes from their own side. A series of votes was then scheduled for 27 July with senators being offered various alternatives. Having lost the first three votes, Senate Majority Leader Mitch McConnell pressed on to the fourth — at 1.24 in the morning of the following day. Just when it looked as if only Murkowski and Collins would vote 'no' — allowing the Vice President to break a 50–50 tie in the Republicans' favour — Senator John McCain of Arizona decided to vote 'no', thereby ensuring the legislation was defeated 49–51. Having boasted of the speed and ease with which he could get a Republican Congress to repeal and replace Obamacare, Trump had to find someone to blame. 'The Democrats have let you down, big league,' Trump complained.

The whole 'repeal and replace' issue returned to the Senate in late September with the so-called Cassidy–Graham bill, sponsored by two Republican senators — Bill Cassidy of Louisiana and Lindsey Graham of South Carolina. But this crashed on take-off as within a few days Republican senators John McCain, Rand Paul and Susan Collins all said they would not support it, with a couple of other Republicans sounding very doubtful — more humiliation for Senate Majority Leader Mitch McConnell and the President.

There were other ways in which Congress used its checks on President Trump. In late July, both houses of Congress gave final passage to a bill imposing sweeping new sanctions on Russia as well as sharply limiting the president's power to suspend new and existing sanctions. Trump had threatened to veto the legislation but given the votes by which it passed in both chambers — 419–3 in the House and 98–2 in the Senate — the President wisely decided that a veto would have been futile.

So what does all this tell us about the effectiveness of congressional checks on the presidency in the Trump era? The answer to that is 'probably less than one might at first think'. Although there may be evidence that Congress's investigative checks on the president are alive and well, the other examples in this section may tell us more about President Trump's lack of connection with his own party in Congress than about the health of checks and balances. Trump was elected in 2016 *despite* being the Republican on the ticket. He didn't so much run for his party's nomination as go against the party establishment in something resembling a hostile takeover. It is therefore hardly surprising that Trump now has few true friends and allies on Capitol Hill, even among Republicans. Furthermore, a president whose approval ratings are stuck in the low 40 and high 30 percentages fails to have the political clout of one who is riding high in public approval — especially one who also lost the popular vote by almost 3 million votes.

As for the checks and balances, we will discover how well those are operating only if the Trump presidency really runs into trouble — if the economy collapses, if the country faces a major foreign threat or a dramatic event of domestic terrorism, if any of the various investigators find evidence that the President colluded with the Russians, if Trump fires the special counsel (see Chapter 4) and other top Department of Justice officials, if Trump pardons everyone involved, and then pardons himself — then we shall find out whether the Constitution really works.

Questions

1 Explain why the Founding Fathers thought the power of the executive branch needed to be checked?
2 Read James Madison's views as expressed in the extract in Box 1.1. Put these views into your own words.
3 What were the major provisions of Executive Order 13769?
4 Explain how and why the federal courts blocked this order.
5 What was President Trump's reaction to the blocking of his order by the courts?
6 What does the author mean when he says that the President was 'hoisted by his own petard' (p. 4)?
7 What do these events tell us about judicial checks on the president?
8 Why did President Trump's attempts to repeal and replace Obamacare fail?
9 Why did the three Republican House members in Table 1.1 have no real incentive to support the President?
10 How did Congress check the President regarding sanctions on Russia?

Chapter 2

To what extent can a president reshape the Supreme Court?

What you need to know

- The Supreme Court is the highest federal court in the USA.
- The Court is made up of nine justices, appointed by the president for life, but subject to confirmation by the Senate.
- The Supreme Court has the power of judicial review. This is the power to declare Acts of Congress, or actions of the executive branch — or acts or actions of state governments — unconstitutional, and thereby null and void.

Why so important?

In his autobiography *A Time To Heal*, Gerald Ford (president 1974–77) wrote:

> Few appointments a president makes can have as much impact on the future of the country as those to the Supreme Court. The opinions of those selected affect the course of our society and the lives of our citizens for generations to come.

Ford wrote this of the time in 1975 when he was about to make his one and only appointment to the Supreme Court — that of John Paul Stevens to replace the ailing William O. Douglas who had served on the Court for more than 36 years. So why are the appointments that a president makes to the Supreme Court often said to be the most important and significant of a presidency?

First, as Ford himself acknowledges, the Supreme Court is an extraordinarily important institution within the US system of government with its intricate set of checks and balances between the three branches of the federal government. Second, members of the Court enjoy life tenure and therefore may remain on the Court for years — possibly decades after the president leaves office, even sometimes after he dies. President Ford appointed Stevens to the Court in 1975 but in less than 2 years, Ford was out of office — defeated by Jimmy Carter in the 1976 election. When Ford died in 2006, aged 93, Stevens was still on the Court, serving until he retired in 2010 having served for just short of 35 years.

Furthermore, a justice of the Supreme Court is one of nine people. Decisions can be made with the agreement of just five justices, and therefore by appointing just one member, the president is choosing someone who, with the agreement of four other people, can make landmark decisions that may change the shape of American government and society for decades — even centuries — to come.

But if all justices were the same in the way they thought and made decisions, then who the president appointed would matter hardly at all. But, of course, different justices have very different judicial philosophies — the basic beliefs that a justice brings to their judicial decision-making. To simplify things, we tend to describe a justice as being either a 'strict constructionist' or a 'loose constructionist' (see Box 2.1). Republican presidents tend to appoint the former, while Democrats tend to appoint the latter.

> ### Box 2.1 Judicial philosophy explained
>
> **Strict constructionist** — a justice who interprets the Constitution in a strict or literal fashion, who tends to favour devolving decision-making to the state governments.
>
> **Loose constructionist** — a justice who interprets the Constitution in a loose or less literal fashion, who tends to favour the centralisation of decision-making in the federal government.

All that having been said, we now address the question, 'To what extent can a president reshape the Supreme Court?' The line of argument we will follow is that for a president to be able to reshape the philosophy of the Court, four factors have to be in place.

Reshaping the Court in practice

1 A vacancy must occur

This may sound obvious, but it is worth stating. Of the 44 people who have thus far served as president, four were never able to appoint anyone to the Court as no vacancy occurred during their term of office (see Table 2.1). Of these four, only Jimmy Carter served a full term in office and therefore must be regarded as the most unlucky in this respect.

Table 2.1 Presidents who made no appointments to the Supreme Court

President	Term of office
William Harrison	4 March — 4 April 1841
Zachary Taylor	4 March 1849 — 9 July 1850
Andrew Johnson	15 April 1885 — 4 March 1869
Jimmy Carter	20 January 1977 — 20 January 1981

At the other end of the scale, George Washington obviously appointed the most (11), as he was able to appoint the original six members of the Court in 1789 plus five replacement justices. Franklin D. Roosevelt appointed nine justices during his just over 12 years in office. But luckiest of all in this respect was William Howard Taft (1909–13), who in his 4-year term appointed five justices to the Court as well as elevating Justice Edward D. White to be chief justice. Modern-day presidents (see Table 2.2) have had around two or three vacancies on the Court during a two-term presidency.

Table 2.2 Number of Supreme Court vacancies by presidencies, 1969–2017

President/party	Years in office	Supreme Court vacancies
Richard Nixon (R)	5½	4
Gerald Ford (R)	2½	1
Jimmy Carter (D)	4	0
Ronald Reagan (R)	8	4
George H. W. Bush (R)	4	2
Bill Clinton (D)	8	2
George W. Bush (R)	8	2
Barack Obama (D)	8	3

2 The nominee must be of a different judicial philosophy from their predecessor

This is an important and oft-forgotten factor, for merely filling a vacancy on the Court does not of itself change the Court's philosophical balance. That is possible only if the president chooses a replacement who is of a distinctly different judicial philosophy from their predecessor. If we consider the nine current members of the Court, to what extent did they fulfil this factor? Table 2.3 suggests that in the appointment of six of these nine, the president was merely appointing a justice of roughly the same philosophy as their predecessor and was not thereby changing the shape of the Court.

Table 2.3 Current Supreme Court justices: did their appointment change the philosophy of the Court?

President	Incumbent	Replacement	Change in philosophy?
Reagan	Lewis Powell	Anthony Kennedy	No
Bush (41)	Thurgood Marshall	Clarence Thomas	Yes
Clinton	Bryon White	Ruth Bader Ginsburg	Yes
Clinton	Harry Blackmun	Stephen Breyer	No
Bush (43)	William Rehnquist	John Roberts	No
Bush (43)	Sandra Day O'Connor	Samuel Alito	Yes
Obama	David Souter	Sonia Sotomayor	No
Obama	John Paul Stevens	Elena Kagan	No
Trump	Antonin Scalia	Neil Gorsuch	No

Now obviously in Table 2.3 we are making some generalisations as to the justices' philosophy. If quoting this argument in an essay, you would need to issue that health warning at the start. But, that said, even allowing for such broad generalisations it is fairly clear that on most occasions during the past three decades — Anthony Kennedy joined the Court exactly 30 years ago in 1988 — the president was not likely to change the philosophical balance of the Court by making the appointment he did. On six of the nine occasions, the president merely replaced like with like.

But three presidents — both Bushes and Bill Clinton — did try to rebalance the Court in at least one of their Supreme Court nominations.

The most clear example of this was George H. W. Bush's appointment of Clarence Thomas to replace Thurgood Marshall in 1991. By this appointment, Bush replaced the most liberal member on the Court with the person who would immediately become the most conservative member of the Court. Thomas's appointment to replace Marshall led to an immediate and significant change in the philosophical balance of the Court and heralded a quarter of a century of conservative domination of the Court.

The other two examples may have been less dramatic but were nonetheless quite significant. Bryon White had been appointed by President Kennedy in 1962, but disappointed his more liberal supporters by taking a more centrist position on the Court, one that did not clearly follow any specific judicial philosophy. But in some landmark decisions — notably in *Roe* v *Wade* in 1973 — White sided with the conservative wing of the Court. Therefore, when Bill Clinton filled the vacancy by appointing Ruth Bader Ginsburg — a clear loose constructionist, liberal justice — Clinton was able to tilt the balance of the Court in the direction of its liberal minority. And Ginsburg has probably become more liberal during her quarter-century on the Court thereby further enhancing the philosophical shift that President Clinton had hoped for.

When Sandra Day O'Connor retired in 2005, George W. Bush replaced her with Samuel Alito. By so doing, Bush was replacing a justice who meandered between conservative and more centrist positions with one who was an out-and-out strict constructionist. The significance of the Alito for O'Connor switch was seen in the Supreme Court's 2007 decision in *Gonzales* v *Carhart* in which the Court upheld the Partial-Birth Abortion Ban Act (2003) in a 5–4 decision in which Alito's vote was decisive. But back in 2000, in *Stenberg* v *Carhart*, the Court had struck down a Nebraska state law prohibiting the same late-term procedure. In that case, O'Connor had sided with the Court's four liberal justices to author a majority opinion which, while recognising the procedure could be 'gruesome', nonetheless decided that it was sometimes necessary. So here was an example where a president's Supreme Court appointment had resulted in a clear change of mind by the Court.

3 The Senate must be willing to confirm the nominee

All nominations by the president to the Supreme Court are subject to confirmation by the Senate by a simple majority vote. Of the 151 nominations made from George Washington to Donald Trump, the Senate has confirmed 124 of them — an impressive 82%. But that leaves 27 nominations that for one reason or another fell by the wayside. As Figure 2.1 shows, 12 of those were rejected by the Senate, 10 were withdrawn and on the remaining five nominations the Senate took no action.

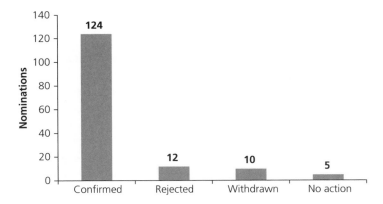

Figure 2.1 Action taken on Supreme Court nominations, 1789–2017

Nine of the twelve rejections came between 1795 and 1930. Grover Cleveland even managed to have two nominees rejected in the same year – 1894. There have been just three rejections in the past 50 years: two Nixon nominees – Clement Haynsworth (1969) and Harrold Carswell (1970) – and Reagan nominee Robert Bork (1987). Had Bork been confirmed in 1987 to replace Justice Lewis Powell, it would certainly have swung the Court much further to the conservative side. As it was, the vacancy was filled by Anthony Kennedy, a justice with a very similar voting record to his predecessor.

Ten nominations have been withdrawn before the Senate voted on them. The most recent example was the withdrawal of the nomination of Harriet Miers by George W. Bush in 2005. Miers withdrew from consideration after Republican as well as Democratic senators questioned her qualification and suitability for the post.

On five occasions, the Senate took no action on the president's nominee. Most recently, this occurred with President Obama's nomination of Judge Merrick Garland in 2016. Obama nominated Garland on 16 March to fill the vacancy created by the sudden death of Justice Antonin Scalia the previous month. But for over 9 months, the Republican majority in the Senate refused even to hold hearings on Garland's nomination, which expired in January of 2017. The vacancy was eventually filled by President Trump nominee Judge Neil Gorsuch. Had Garland replaced Scalia, it would clearly have tilted the Court towards a more centrist/liberal path. But the Garland fiasco showed the importance of this third factor being in place if a president hopes to reshape the Supreme Court.

4 The justice must turn out as expected

But there is one more factor that must be in place – that the justice must turn out as expected. For there have been instances when all the first three factors have been in place but because the nominee has not turned out as expected, the president's desire to reshape the Court has not been fulfilled. This has occurred twice in the past 50 years – President Ford's nomination of John Paul Stevens in 1975, and President George H. W. Bush's nomination of David Souter in 1990. In both cases, the president thought he was appointing a conservative, strict constructionist, but both nominees then put together a voting record on the Court that was solidly in the loose constructionist mould and were reliable liberal votes on the Court.

When Ford was looking for a nominee to fill the 1975 vacancy, his Attorney General Edward Levi — a close confidant of the President — assured him that 'Stevens is generally a moderate conservative in his approach to judicial problems'. But by the 1990s, Stevens was the most reliably liberal voice on the Court. He had clearly changed since joining the Court. One policy area in which Stevens changed was the death penalty (see Box 2.2), and another was affirmative action. On affirmative action, Stevens had co-authored an opinion with conservative justices in 1978 that held that racial quotas were unconstitutional, but in 1995 he wrote an opinion with liberal justices that racial quotas were constitutional.

Box 2.2 | **Justice Stevens changes his views on the death penalty**

- *Gregg* v *Georgia* (1976) — Stevens voted with the majority to reinstate the death penalty after a 4-year moratorium.
- *Kansas* v *Marsh* (2006) — Stevens in dissenting minority in a decision that upheld Kansas's death penalty law.
- *Baze* v *Rees* (2008) — Stevens dissented in a decision upholding Kentucky's lethal injection procedure as constitutional.

Extract from Justice Stevens' dissent in *Baze* v *Rees*:

> I have reached the conclusion that the imposition of the death penalty represents the pointless and needless extinction of life with only marginal contributions to any discernible social or public purpose. A penalty with such negligible returns to the State is patently a 'cruel and unusual punishment'.

Conclusion

To sum up, four factors need to be in place if a president is to reshape the Supreme Court. So it is a lot more sophisticated than suggesting that all presidents who make a nomination to the Supreme Court can change the Court's judicial philosophy. Mostly, they can't. Of recent presidents, only three have. But for those who do it is a significant prize, and maybe the most important part of their legacy.

Questions

1 Why are appointments to the Supreme Court so important?
2 Explain the difference between strict and loose constructionist justices.
3 What does Table 2.2 show about the frequency of Supreme Court vacancies?
4 How did the nominations of Clarence Thomas, Ruth Bader Ginsburg and Samuel Alito change the shape of the Supreme Court?
5 Give some recent examples of some Supreme Court nominees who were not confirmed by the Senate.
6 Why did Merrick Garland fail to become a justice of the Supreme Court?
7 What does Box 2.2 tell us about Justice Stevens' evolving views on the death penalty?

Chapter 3

The Supreme Court: the 2016–17 term

What you need to know

- The Supreme Court is the highest court in the USA.
- The Court is made up of nine justices, appointed by the president, for life.
- This said, for most of the 2016–17 term, the Court had only eight members.
- The Supreme Court has the power of judicial review: the power to declare Acts of Congress or actions of the executive branch — or acts or actions of state governments — unconstitutional, and thereby null and void.
- By this power of judicial review, the Court acts as the umpire of the Constitution and plays a leading role in safeguarding Americans' rights and liberties.

This was the second consecutive Supreme Court during which for much of the time the Court had only eight members. Following the death of Antonin Scalia in February 2016, the Republican-controlled Senate refused to consider President Obama's nomination of Merrick Garland to fill the vacancy. Therefore the Court was one justice short from February 2016 until April 2017 when the Senate confirmed President Trump's nominee Neil Gorsuch. This was an unprecedented length of time for the Court to be short of its full complement. It meant that the last 4 months of the 2015–16 term and the first 6 months of the 2016–17 term were conducted with just eight justices on the bench, making 4–4 decisions a distinct possibility. By the time Gorsuch joined the Court in April, most of the term's cases had already been argued before the Court and therefore Gorsuch was unable to participate in conversation among his colleagues on the outcome. Gorsuch joined the Court on 9 April 2017, but did not participate in a decision until 5 June. During the whole term, Gorsuch participated in just 16 cases, authoring only one opinion, which was a unanimous decision of the Court announced on 12 June. For this reason, our regular analysis of the Court in terms of 5–4 decisions, and the balance between the so-called conservative and liberal wings of the Court is more problematic.

Table 3.1 Significant Supreme Court decisions, 2016–17 term

Case	Concerning	Decision
Trinity Lutheran Church of Columbia v *Comer*	Separation of church and state	7–2
Moore v *Texas*	Death penalty	5–3

Because it was known that the Court would be one justice short, a number of likely pending controversial cases did not appear on the Court's list when the term opened in October 2016. So it was no surprise that the 2016–17 term was not one marked by a large number of highly controversial or landmark decisions. In this chapter we shall consider two of the Court's decisions relating to areas of the Court's jurisdiction that we have considered before — freedom of religion and capital punishment.

The Court and the separation of church and state

The First Amendment begins:

> Congress shall make no law respecting an establishment of religion, or prohibiting the free exercise thereof.

Over recent decades, the Supreme Court has struggled to act as umpire between these two conflicting requirements. Critics of the Court have often suggested that the Court has been much more careful to safeguard the first half of that provision, to the detriment of the second half. Put another way, the Court has been careful to keep a strict separation between church and state, even if that meant people's individual rights to practise their religion in the public forum have been partially curtailed.

First, the background to this case — *Trinity Lutheran Church of Columbia* v *Comer*. Columbia is a town in Missouri of some 120,000 people just south of Interstate 70 as it runs east–west between St Louis and Kansas City. In 2012, Trinity Lutheran Church applied for a grant under a state-sponsored programme to use recycled tyres to resurface a playground on the church campus. The idea of the Missouri programme was to help organisations make playgrounds safer. But the Missouri Constitution bars spending public money 'directly or indirectly, in aid of any church', and the state Supreme Court had called for 'a very high wall between church and state'. Not that this provision in Missouri's Constitution is unusual — 38 other states have similar provisions. When the church's application for a grant on the recycling programme was turned down, it was rejected solely because of the religious nature of the organisation — because it is a church. As Chief Justice Roberts wrote in his majority opinion:

> In this case, there is no dispute that Trinity Lutheran is put to the choice between being a church and receiving a government benefit. The rule is simple: No churches need apply.

In a 7–2 decision — with Justices Sonia Sotomayor and Ruth Bader Ginsburg dissenting — the Supreme Court ruled that states must provide aid to religious groups even when their state constitutions call for a strict separation of church and state. Although seven justices signed the majority opinion, they differed about how broadly the Court should have ruled. For example, Chief Justice Roberts added a footnote to the majority opinion that limited the sweep and scope of the opinion.

> This case involves express discrimination based on religious identity with respect to playground resurfacing. We do not address religious uses of funding or other forms of discrimination.

Two justices in particular — Clarence Thomas and Neil Gorsuch — thought this overly narrowed the decision and refused to endorse this footnote. In this partial break with the majority and in his lining up with Justice Thomas, Justice Gorsuch showed an early indication that he may well live up to the very conservative views of his predecessor Antonin Scalia (see Box 3.1). It also shows different justices working in different ways on the Court. Chief Justice Roberts wherever possible wants to make narrow, limited decisions with the aim of building as wide a consensus for them as possible. Roberts believes, for example, that a 7–2 decision such as this one carries more weight than a 5–4 decision. Justice Gorsuch, on the other hand, seems to favour decisions that are more broad and wide-ranging even if that means losing other justices' support along the way.

Box 3.1	**Extract from Justice Gorsuch's opinion in _Trinity Lutheran_ v _Comer_**

I worry that some might mistakenly read [Chief Justice Roberts's footnote] to suggest that only 'playground resurfacing' cases, or only those with some association with children's safety or health, or perhaps some other social good we find sufficiently worthy, are governed by the legal rules recounted in and faithfully applied by the Court's opinion. Such a reading would be unreasonable, for our cases are governed by general principles rather than ad hoc improvisations. And the general principles here do not permit discrimination against religious exercise — whether on the playground or anywhere else.

Not only did the Chief Justice manage to keep Thomas and Gorsuch on board — who would have liked the decision to have gone further — he also did enough to keep Justice Stephen Breyer on board too. Breyer, who voted with the majority but did not agree with their reasoning, said he would have preferred an even narrower decision.

Box 3.2	**Extract from Justice Sotomayor's opinion in _Trinity Lutheran_ v _Comer_**

The church has a religious mission, one that it pursues through the learning center. The playground surface cannot be confined to secular use any more than lumber used to frame the church's walls... or nails to build its altar. The constitutional provisions of 39 states — all but invalidated today — the weighty interests they protect, and the history they draw on deserve more than this judicial brush aside. In the end, the soundness of today's decision may matter less than what it might enable tomorrow. The principle it establishes can be manipulated to call for a similar fate for lines drawn on the basis of religious use.

This case was also affected by the unexpected death of Justice Scalia in February 2016. The Court had agreed to hear the case just a few weeks before Scalia's death. Fearing deadlock in an eight-member court, the decision was made to delay oral argument in the case until the Court once again had a full complement of justices. It was eventually argued in April 2017, soon after Justice Gorsuch joined the Court.

So what effect did this decision have, and what further effect may it have in the future? Almost immediately after the judgement, the Republican Governor of Missouri Eric Greitens announced that the state would no longer discriminate against religious groups in evaluating grant applications for programmes such as the one involved in this case. But potentially, the effect of the case could be quite far-reaching and go well beyond school playground safety. Many commentators saw this decision as a game-changer in the long-running debate over whether public money could be used to give parents school vouchers for use in private, religious schools. Michael Bindas, senior attorney at the Institute of Justice, claimed that the *Trinity Lutheran* decision 'shows the Court takes the principle of neutrality toward religion in public benefit programmes very seriously'. In his majority opinion, Chief Justice Roberts held that the Missouri ruling against offering a grant to the church 'expressly discriminates against otherwise eligible recipients by disqualifying them from a public benefit solely because of their religious character'. Bindas called this 'a tremendous development for school choice'.

Secretary of Education Betsy DeVos celebrated the *Trinity* decision as a victory for the school choice movement which sees the Trump administration — and now the Supreme Court — as favourably disposed to its ideas. Indeed, the President's first budget featured a $1.4 billion school choice package that includes millions of dollars that low-income families could use to send their children to private, religious schools. This decision was the one potential landmark ruling of this term.

The death penalty

The Court has made a number of significant decisions concerning the use of the death penalty and how that relates to the Eighth Amendment's ban on 'cruel and unusual punishments'. Even in this century, the Court has ruled twice on the use of lethal injection — *Baze v Rees* (2008) and *Glossip v Gross* (2015) — as well as two further rulings on mental disability, in *Atkins v Virginia* (2002) and *Hall v Florida* (2014). The Court's decision in *Moore v Texas* was related to the later two cases.

In the *Atkins* decision in 2002, the Court had ruled that executing those who were mentally disabled violated the Eighth Amendment. The trouble was that the Court did not define what it meant by mental disability. Twelve years later, the Court also declared a Florida state law unconstitutional because it set a fixed IQ score — 70 — above which people could be executed, but below which they could not. In this later decision in 2014, the Court ruled that states must take into consideration the IQ test's standard margin of error — usually +/– 5 points.

In April 1980, Bobby Moore, along with two accomplices, conducted an armed robbery on a supermarket in Houston, Texas. Moore shot and killed an employee, was arrested, convicted of murder and sentenced to death. But Moore then spent decades fighting his case through the courts claiming he had a mental disability.

In a 5–3 decision, the Court held that executing Moore would be unconstitutional because the IQ testing used by Texas was regarded by many experts as being out of date and unreliable. The majority opinion was written by Justice Ginsburg, joined by fellow liberal justices Breyer, Sotomayor and Kagan, along with Justice Anthony Kennedy. In his dissent, Chief Justice Roberts – joined by fellow conservatives Clarence Thomas and Samuel Alito – criticised his colleagues for having made their decision 'based solely on what [they] deem to be medical consensus about intellectual disability' (see Box 3.3). But this decision was significant in that it marked yet another nibbling away at death penalty provisions.

Box 3.3	Extract from Chief Justice Roberts's dissenting opinion in *Moore* v *Texas*

Clinicians, not judges, should determine clinical standards; and judges, not clinicians, should determine the content of the Eighth Amendment. Today's opinion confuses those roles, and therefore I respectfully dissent.

Overview of the 2016–17 term

If one had to sum up the 2016–17 term in two words they would be 'caution' and 'consensus.' As Justice Alito explained:

> Having eight justices was unusual and awkward. That probably required having a lot more discussion of some things and more compromise and maybe narrower opinions than we would have issued otherwise.

This partly resulted from a lack of contentious and divisive cases. Look out for a larger than usual number of those coming up in the 2017–18 term. The Court has already agreed to hear cases on a clash between gay rights and religious freedom, gerrymandering and mobile phone privacy. With Gorsuch now in place, the Court is hoping to make up for those 14 months when they were one member down. William Baude, a law professor at the University of Chicago commented: 'It has been a quieter term, and that is a good thing for the country, but we may look back on this term as the calm before the storm.'

Table 3.2 Total, unanimous and 5–4 decisions: 2011–17

Term:	2011–12	2012–13	2013–14	2014–15	2015–16	2016–17
Number of decisions	75	78	72	75	76	69
Percentage which were unanimous	44%	49%	65%	40%	50%	59%
Percentage which were 5–4 decisions	20%	29%	14%	26%	5%	10%

Even the workload was down this term with just 69 decisions – the lowest figure for 10 years and well below the average of 76 for the past twelve terms. As recently as 2009–10, the Court handed down 86 decisions in a term. The Court scored highly for unanimity with 59% of decisions being unanimous compared with 50% in the previous term. The percentage of 5–4 (or 5–3) decisions was very low at just 10%, but as with the previous term, this was mostly due to the Court having only eight members for much of the time.

In such 5–4 and 5–3 decisions that there were in this term, the liberal quartet plus Justice Kennedy were more often than not in the majority, with the conservative trio of Roberts, Thomas and Alito in the minority – later joined by Gorsuch. With the Court's conservative wing remaining depleted for much of the term, it was hardly surprising that the Court's liberal wing found it easier to put together a majority. As Figure 3.1 shows, the conservatives plus Kennedy were in the majority in only 29% of 5–4 or 5–3 decisions in this term, making this the third consecutive term when the liberal wing of the Court has been more successful in closely contested decisions.

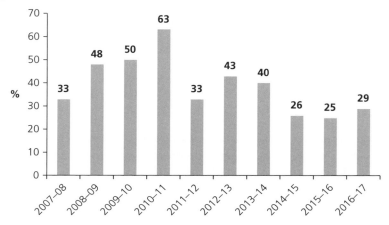

Figure 3.1 Percentage of 5–4 or 5–3 decisions in which the conservative quartet were in the majority, 2007–17

For the second successive term, the two justices most often in agreement were Reagan appointee Anthony Kennedy and Obama appointee Elena Kagan, which does suggest that after just 6 years on the Court, Kagan is proving to be much more of a centrist than the justice whom she replaced – John Paul Stevens. Also for the second successive year, justices Thomas and Ginsburg were the two justices most in disagreement, placing them at opposite ends of the Court's philosophical spectrum (see Table 3.3).

Table 3.3 Agreement and disagreement between justices, 2011–17

Term:	2011–12	2012–13	2013–14	2014–15	2015–16	2016–17
Two justices most in agreement	Scalia Thomas	Ginsburg Kagan	Thomas Alito	Breyer Ginsburg	Kennedy Kagan	Kennedy Kagan
Two justices most in disagreement	Scalia Ginsburg	Alito Ginsburg	Alito Sotomayor	Thomas Sotomayor	Thomas Ginsburg	Thomas Ginsburg

The Court's statistics also show us that the justices conduct themselves differently in their work. Some work quicker than others when it comes to writing their opinions. As Figure 3.2 shows, whereas Justice Sotomayor took an average of just 67 days to write her opinions, fellow Obama appointee Justice Kagan took an average of 108 days.

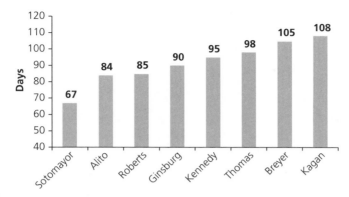

Figure 3.2 Average number of days between oral argument and majority opinion

Yet again, Justice Kennedy was the justice most often in the majority — in 97% of cases. He has now held this distinction either individually or jointly for eight of the past nine terms (see Table 3.4). Kennedy was also the justice most frequently in the majority in 5–4 and 5–3 decisions.

Table 3.4 Justice(s) most often in the majority, by terms (2008–17)

Term	Justice(s) most often in the majority	Percentage
2008–09	Anthony Kennedy	92
2009–10	Anthony Kennedy and John Roberts	91
2010–11	Anthony Kennedy	94
2011–12	Anthony Kennedy	93
2012–13	Anthony Kennedy	91
2013–14	Anthony Kennedy, John Roberts and Elena Kagan	92
2014–15	Stephen Breyer	92
2015–16	Anthony Kennedy	98
2016–17	Anthony Kennedy	97

We also discover that some justices are more vocal in oral argument than others. In this term, the Court divided into four more vociferous members who tended to ask lots of questions at oral arguments and a much quieter quartet who spoke less frequently. During his brief period on the Court towards the end of the term, Justice Gorsuch fell between the two (see Table 3.5, p. 22).

When it comes to asking the first question at oral argument, Justice Ginsburg topped the table asking the first question in 30% of oral arguments, while justices Breyer, Alito and Thomas never asked the first question. Having broken his 10-year silence at oral argument in the previous term, Justice Thomas was again silent this term asking no questions at all at oral argument.

And the future?

There was much speculation on the final day of the Court's term as to whether or not Justice Anthony Kennedy would announce his retirement and thereby give

Table 3.5 Average number of questions at oral argument

Justice	Average number of questions per oral argument
Stephen Breyer	20.5
Sonia Sotomayor	19.6
John Roberts	17.9
Elena Kagan	16.7
Neil Gorsuch	13.7
Anthony Kennedy	10.5
Ruth Bader Ginsburg	10.2
Samuel Alito	10.1
Clarence Thomas	0

President Trump the opportunity to make a second appointment to the Court in his first year. But it was not to be — at least for the time being. Both Ruth Bader Ginsburg (84) and Anthony Kennedy (81) are over 80. Kennedy has now served on the Court for 30 years. It is widely known that the Trump and Kennedy families are quite friendly. If Trump were to be able to name a strict constructionist to replace centrist Anthony Kennedy, Trump would have secured his legacy on the Court. But he would need to do that while the Republicans still control the Senate. On the other hand, Kennedy might prefer to keep the seat with a centrist justice like himself and his predecessor Lewis Powell. If so, an appointment made by a Republican president but confirmed by a Democrat-controlled Senate might fit the bill.

One cannot imagine Justice Ginsburg wanting to have her replacement named by President Trump, so there is every incentive for her to hang on until at least 2021 hoping that a Democrat might be in the White House by then. But will her somewhat frail health hold up? And by 2021, Stephen Breyer — another Clinton appointee — will be 82. It is the naming of the replacements to those three justices — none of them conservatives — that may determine the course of the Supreme Court for the next three decades.

Questions

1 Why did this Supreme Court term lack many landmark decisions?
2 What did the Court decide about the separation of church and state in the *Trinity Lutheran* judgement?
3 Examine the different views as put forward by justices Gorsuch and Sotomayor in the *Trinity Lutheran* decision.
4 In what way did the Supreme Court again 'nibble away' at the death penalty provision in 2017?
5 What do the data presented in Table 3.2 and Figure 3.1 tell us about the Supreme Court in 2016–17?
6 What evidence is presented to suggest that Anthony Kennedy is probably the most influential justice on the Supreme Court?
7 What opportunities might open up for further appointments to the Supreme Court in the next year or so?

Chapter 4

Grand juries, special prosecutors, pardons and impeachment

During President Trump's first year in office, the British media — like their American counterparts — have been using terms with which not even they are entirely familiar. 'Special Counsel Mueller using grand jury' exclaimed the *Washington Post* headline back in mid-August of 2017, while Britain's *Daily Telegraph* reported, 'Grand jury subpoenas Michael Flynn associates'. Not to be left out, the *Independent* headlined, 'Democrat to introduce Trump impeachment articles'. But just what is a grand jury? What is a special counsel? What are impeachment articles? This chapter will help to get you up to speed on investigatory and prosecutorial terminology.

Grand jury

Of all the terms we are going to discuss here, this is one of the most widely misunderstood. The trouble is that in the British judicial system, a jury is what decides guilt or innocence at a trial. And 'grand jury' sounds even more impressive. But it isn't. It is a completely different animal. A grand jury in the US judicial system is a group of people — numbering anything from 12 to 23 — who hear evidence presented in *pre-trial* proceedings to decide whether or not an individual has a criminal case to answer. If the grand jury thinks there is a criminal case to answer, then they indict — formally accuse — that person, and the case will come to court for a full trial. If there is no case to answer, there is no trial and the person goes free. So a grand jury does not decide guilt or innocence, but merely whether or not there is the likelihood of a crime having been committed.

So why use a grand jury? There are three reasons.

1 Because in federal courts, it is often a constitutional requirement. The Fifth Amendment — most famous for its prohibition of self-incrimination — states, 'No person shall be held to answer for a capital, or otherwise infamous crime, unless on an indictment of a Grand Jury'. In other words, in federal court an accusation of a serious crime can be brought only after a grand jury indictment.

2 Because many state courts require it. All states have provision for grand juries, though only about half the states actually use them. However, 22 states require their use under various circumstances.

3 Because a grand jury exercises vast powers, being empowered to subpoena — compel — witnesses and records and to compel testimony to be taken under oath.

Therefore, that an individual is the subject of a grand jury investigation is not an insignificant matter, but it is probably less important than the media — especially in Britain — often suggest.

Special prosecutor

The British media tend to use the term 'special prosecutor', but the correct term is 'special counsel', which immediately makes it sound rather less interesting. On 17 May 2017, the Deputy Attorney General Rod Rosenstein appointed the former FBI Director Robert Mueller as special counsel for the Department of Justice to investigate 'any links and/or coordination between the Russian government and individuals associated with the campaign of President Donald Trump and any matters that arose or may arise directly from the investigation'. The appointment was made by Rosenstein, rather than by Attorney General Jeff Sessions, because Sessions had recused himself from any matters relating to the Trump campaign as Sessions had been involved in that campaign. A recusal is a disqualification from performing legal duties because of a possible conflict of interest.

As special counsel, Mueller has power to issue subpoenas, hire staff, request funding and bring prosecutions to court. On 3 August 2017, Mueller impanelled a grand jury in Washington, DC, to hear pre-trial arguments and to decide on possible criminal prosecutions.

The special counsel is said to be investigating specifically:
- attempts by the Russian government to interfere in the 2016 presidential election
- links between the Trump election campaign and officials of the Russian government
- the substance of a meeting held at Trump Tower, New York, in June 2016 between three senior members of the Trump campaign and others who included Russian lawyer Natalia Veselnitskaya
- possible obstruction of justice committed by the President both in his dealings with FBI Director James Comey and his subsequent firing of Comey in May 2017
- financial dealings of the President and his associates in Russia
- the activities of US Army Lieutenant General Michael Flynn who briefly served as Trump's national security adviser at the start of his administration but was fired by Trump after less than a month in office

All this may come to nothing, or prosecutions involving any of the above-mentioned people may be forthcoming.

Presidential pardons

Article II, Section 2, of the Constitution gives to the president 'the Power to Grant Reprieves and Pardons for Offenses against the United States, except in Cases of Impeachment'. Those few words have generated more controversy and debate than most parts of the Constitution. It was Alexander Hamilton who first suggested to the Philadelphia Convention that it grant the president power to pardon criminals. As this was a power associated with monarchs and would be the only unchecked power the Constitution would grant to the president, it is surprising that the Convention delegates went along with Hamilton's suggestion.

So what was Hamilton's reasoning? He set it out in *Federalist No. 74* as follows:

> The principal argument for the power of pardon is this: in seasons of insurrection or rebellion, there are often critical moments when a well-timed offer of pardon to the insurgents or rebels may restore the tranquillity of the nation.

So the framers saw the president's pardon power being used in the context of domestic disquiet with the president restoring national unity by offering mercy to those, presumably on the losing side, who had committed illegal acts. The framers would presumably have approved, therefore, of presidential pardons following the Civil War or after times of great national upheaval such as the protests surrounding America's participation in the Vietnam War.

Coming to the presidency in August 1974 by appointment rather than by election, Gerald Ford used the pardon power in an attempt to heal the nation's wounds from both Watergate and the Vietnam War. On the eleventh day of his presidency — 19 August — Ford announced his amnesty plan for some 50,000 Americans who had either illegally evaded the Vietnam draft or had deserted from the war. It was not an unconditional pardon but a programme through which amnesty could be earned. More controversially, on 8 September, Ford announced a 'full, free and absolute pardon' to his predecessor, Richard Nixon, for any crimes he may have committed during his time as president (see Box 4.1, p. 26). As with the Vietnam amnesty programme, Ford expressed his wish to lay to rest the nation's unhappy past. At the time, Ford was widely criticised for his pardon of Nixon. But less than 3 years later, Jimmy Carter — who had only narrowly defeated Ford in the 1976 election — opened his inaugural address with these words: 'For myself and for our Nation, I want to thank my predecessor for all he has done to heal our land'. Twenty-five years later, in August 1999, Ford returned to the White House to be presented with the Medal of Freedom — the highest civilian award in the United States — by President Bill Clinton.

But there were those, even back in the 1780s, who criticised this granting of the power of pardon to the president. Virginia's George Mason thought it ill-advised to give the pardon power to the president who 'may frequently pardon crimes which were advised by himself'. In 2018, that may prove to be a very prescient thought. And Mason would doubtless have not been surprised by the sometimes dodgy dealings of presidents in pardoning friends, cronies, campaign donors, drug dealers and other highly questionable individuals.

But recent presidents have backed off from pardoning individuals caught in administration scandals or cover-ups. Even Nixon refused to pardon White House staff members, including his Chief of Staff Bob Haldeman who pleaded with his former boss to grant him a pardon for his part in the Watergate cover-up. In the 1980s, Ronald Reagan resisted intense lobbying to pardon Oliver North and John Poindexter for their role in the Iran-Contra scandal. Similarly, George W. Bush refused to pardon Vice President Dick Cheney's former Chief of Staff Scooter Libby after Libby was convicted of lying to a grand jury about his involvement in revealing

Box 4.1	**Extract from President Ford's pardon of President Nixon, 8 September 1974**

Proclamation 4311 — Granting pardon to Richard Nixon

September 8, 1974

By the president of the United States of America

A Proclamation

As a result of certain acts or omissions occurring before his resignation from the Office of President, Richard Nixon has become liable to possible indictment and trial for offenses against the United States. Whether or not he shall be so prosecuted depends on findings of the appropriate grand jury and on the discretion of the authorized prosecutor. Should an indictment ensue, the accused shall then be entitled to a fair trial by an impartial jury, as guaranteed to every individual by the Constitution.

It is believed that a trial of Richard Nixon, if it became necessary, could not fairly begin until a year or more has elapsed. In the meantime, the tranquillity to which this nation has been restored by the events of recent weeks could be irreparably lost by the prospects of bringing to trial a former president of the United States. The prospects of such trial will cause prolonged and divisive debate over the propriety of exposing to further punishment and degradation a man who has already paid the unprecedented penalty of relinquishing the highest elective office of the United States.

Now, Therefore, I, Gerald R. Ford, President of the United States, pursuant to the pardon power conferred upon me by Article II, Section 2, of the Constitution, have granted and by these presents do grant a full, free, and absolute pardon unto Richard Nixon for all offenses against the United States which he, Richard Nixon, has committed or may have committed or taken part in during the period from January 20, 1969 through August 9, 1974.

Gerald R. Ford

a CIA agent's name (Valerie Plame) to reporters. Bush did later commute Libby's 30-month jail sentence, but this fell far short of the full pardon for which Cheney had lobbied unrelentingly during the closing days of the Bush administration.

That said, there have been examples of what many regard as the abuse of the pardon power. Maybe the most notorious was Bill Clinton's pardoning of Marc Rich in January 2001. Rich — a financier and businessman — had been convicted in a federal court in 1983 on 65 counts including tax evasion and racketeering but had fled to Switzerland to avoid jail. Rich's wife Denise later gave substantial sums of money to the Democratic Party (over $1 million), to Hillary Clinton's 2000 Senate campaign (over $100,000) and to the Clinton Foundation Library (nearly half a million dollars). Then, just hours before leaving office, President Clinton pardoned Mr Rich. In his subsequent autobiography (*My Life*, 2004) Bill Clinton offered a half-apology, saying that 'I may have made a mistake' in the pardon of Marc Rich.

In August 2017, President Trump used his pardon power for the first time to controversially pardon former Arizona sheriff Joe Arpaio. While most presidents have left their more controversial pardons to their last months – often the last days – in office, Trump issued his having served just 7 months in the Oval Office. Arpaio had supported Trump throughout his presidential campaign being rewarded with a speaking slot at the party's national convention in 2016. Back in 2011, Arpaio had been warned by a US district judge to stop detaining people he believed to be illegal immigrants when they had not been charged with any crime. But the sheriff continued the policy and was subsequently charged with contempt of court. Arpaio had been found guilty in federal court and when Trump pardoned him was still awaiting sentencing. The President described Arpaio as a 'great American patriot' who had 'done a lot in the fight against illegal immigration'. The pardon raised questions in many people's minds about whether this was meant as a signal to other friends of Trump that they could count on him to pardon them if they got into difficulties with the courts.

That said, for all the recent controversies about pardons, the rate of presidential pardons has decreased markedly since the days of Dwight Eisenhower, Lyndon Johnson or Gerald Ford (see Figure 4.1). Beginning with President Reagan in 1981, recent presidents have used the power much more sparingly, although not necessarily less controversially.

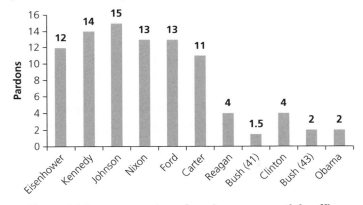

Figure 4.1 Average number of pardons per month in office

So what if Trump were to start pardoning individuals who had committed crimes in connection with his own election campaign or in the White House? The bottom line here, as Richard Ellis (*The Development of the American Presidency*, 2012) puts it:

> A president may abuse the pardon power – as Bill Clinton certainly did in pardoning Marc Rich – but the Constitution undoubtedly gives the president that power. A presidential pardon may obstruct the law or be used to corrupt ends but it cannot be illegal or unconstitutional, so long as it is employed for 'Offences against the United States, except in Cases of Impeachment.'

Which brings us to our final piece of judicial terminology – impeachment.

Impeachment

Here is another term which is widely misunderstood. So first of all, let's get two facts absolutely clear. First, Richard Nixon *was not* impeached. He resigned before the House of Representatives got around to impeaching him. Second, Bill Clinton *was* impeached. The House passed two articles of impeachment against him – the first for perjury to a grand jury, the second for obstruction of justice. But when Clinton was tried on those two articles by the Senate, he was found not guilty on both.

Impeachment is a formal accusation of a federal government official – in this case, the president – by a simple majority vote in the House of Representatives. The case of impeachment is then tried by the Senate. If the president is found guilty by a two-thirds majority, the president is removed from office. That is why Bill Clinton, though impeached, remained in office to complete his second term.

The trouble with impeachment – especially of the president – is that rather than being strictly a matter of fitness for office, it quickly becomes a partisan matter in which members of Congress from the president's party vote 'no' on impeachment and 'not guilty' in the trial, while members from the opposite party vote 'yes' on impeachment and 'guilty' in the trial – almost regardless of the merits, or otherwise, of the case. The reason why President Nixon resigned in 1974 was because he realised that many senators from his own Republican Party would vote 'guilty' in the Senate trial – joining the 56 Democrats – and thereby he would be removed from office.

So, looking at President Trump's position, short of his having committed some heinous crime, he will regard himself as safe from impeachment for so long as the Republicans control both houses of Congress. Furthermore, as the Senate is likely to remain under Republican control or possibly with a small Democratic majority for the last 2 years of this term (2019–20), the President would regard himself as safe in office even were a Democrat-controlled House to pass articles of impeachment against him. So from that viewpoint, ignore all the media chatter about impeachment and removing Trump from office – unless the President is proved to have been involved in some very serious crime or cover-up. Therefore Trump looks fairly certain to remain in office through to at least 20 January 2021. He might face a challenge from within his party in the 2020 Republican primaries. He might lose that year's November election to the Democratic Party's nominee – whoever he or she is. But that's all for another time of writing.

Questions

1 What is a grand jury? Why are they used?
2 Explain the role of Special Counsel Robert Mueller.
3 What arguments for and against the president being given the power of pardon were put forward at the Philadelphia Convention?
4 Why did President Ford offer a possible route to amnesty for Vietnam draft dodgers and deserters? Why did he pardon his predecessor Richard Nixon?
5 Give examples of when recent presidents have been reluctant to pardon people who had served in their administrations.
6 Why was President Clinton's pardon of Marc Rich so controversial?
7 Why did President Trump's pardon of Joe Arpaio cause controversy?
8 What does Figure 4.1 show us about the use of presidential pardons?
9 Why does the author think that President Trump's impeachment is very unlikely?

Chapter 5

More from the 2016 elections

Pretty much the whole of the 2017 edition of this publication was devoted to the 2016 election. But because it went to press very soon after Election Day, we missed presenting some data which was not available at that time.

The popular vote

In terms of the popular vote, Hillary Clinton defeated Donald Trump by just under 3 million votes (see Table 5.1) with Clinton capturing 48.2% of the popular vote and Trump gaining 46.1%. However, what is obscured by those headline figures is that there was a difference in the two candidates' votes between the swing states and the safe states. In the thirteen swing states, Trump beat Clinton by almost 1 million votes – 48.3% to 46.6%. But in the safe, or non-swing states, Trump did much less well, losing to Clinton by 4 percentage points, 49% to 45%. It was also true that third-party and independent candidates did less well in the swing states (5.1%) than in the non-swing states (6%).

Table 5.1 Popular vote totals, 2016

Candidate:	Donald Trump (R)	Hillary Clinton (D)	Other candidates
Nationwide	62,984,824	**65,853,516**	7,801,446
Nationwide (%)	46.1%	**48.2%**	5.7%
Swing states	**22,249,342**	21,433,214	2,348,069
Swing states (%)	**48.3%**	46.6%	5.1%
Non-swing states	40,735,482	**44,420,302**	5,453,377
Non-swing states (%)	45%	**49%**	6%

Winner in bold

Put another way, nationwide there was a swing to the Republicans of just under 2% from 2012. However, while the Republicans enjoyed a swing of between 5% and 6% in the swing states, in the non-swing states there was actually a very small swing to the Democrats. Three of the five states in which the Republicans enjoyed their biggest swings were swing states – Iowa (+15), Maine (+12) and Ohio (+11). By contrast, the Democrats had their biggest swings in California – which they won by 30 percentage points anyway – and in Utah which they lost by nearly 20 percentage points. The moral of the story on the popular vote was that the Republicans got their votes where it counted most, while the Democrats ended up with a huge number of wasted votes. And that partly explains what happened in the Electoral College, of which we will say more later.

Another issue relating to the popular vote that went largely unreported was that 2016 represented the sixth election out of the last seven – that's going back to 1992 – in which the Democrats won the popular vote (Table 5.2). The only election since 1992 in which the Republicans won the popular vote was in 2004. This shows the significant difficulty the Republicans are having in putting together a winning popular vote coalition. With the non-Hispanic white population forecast to decline by a further 17% by 2060 from its 2015 level, the Republicans will find it only more challenging in future elections, especially as the Hispanic vote is forecast to increase by 65% over the same period.

Table 5.2 Popular vote for two major parties: 1992–2016

Year	Democratic vote (%)	Republican vote (%)
1992	**43.1**	37.5
1996	**49.2**	40.7
2000	**48.4**	47.9
2004	48.3	**50.7**
2008	**52.9**	45.7
2012	**51.1**	47.2
2016	**48.2**	46.1

Winner in bold

Third-party votes

The most significant part played by a third party in the 2016 presidential race was that played by Libertarian Party candidate Gary Johnson, the former Republican governor of New Mexico. Johnson teamed up with another ex-Republican governor, William Weld of Massachusetts, as his running mate. The Johnson–Weld ticket received just under 4.5 million votes, representing 3.3% of the national vote, the highest percentage of the popular vote for a third-party candidate since Ross Perot's 8.4% for the Reform Party in 1996. But did Johnson in any way affect the final outcome of the election? Did he help elect Donald Trump? Those kinds of questions are always difficult to answer as we have no way of knowing how Johnson voters would have voted had he not been standing, or even if they would have voted at all. After the results were published, some attention was given to those four states in which Johnson's votes exceeded the margin by which Trump had defeated Clinton – Florida, Michigan, Pennsylvania and Wisconsin – which between them commanded 75 electoral votes (see Table 5.3). With Clinton ending 43 electoral votes short of the 270 required for an overall majority, she would have won the election had she secured certain combinations of two or three of those states. There was certainly some evidence that Johnson was attracting anti-Clinton Democrats – the supporters of Bernie Sanders in the Democratic primaries.

Table 5.3 Votes for leading candidates in states in which Johnson's vote was greater than the margin between Trump winning and Clinton losing

State	Trump vote	Clinton vote	Johnson vote
Florida	4,617,886	4,504,975	297,178
Michigan	2,279,543	2,268,839	250,902
Pennsylvania	2,970,733	2,926,441	218,228
Wisconsin	1,405,284	1,382,536	188,330

But of course Johnson might have also been attracting anti-Trump Republicans, though the polling done before Election Day showed this to be a less fruitful field for the Libertarian ticket.

The other noteworthy performance by a third-party candidate was that of Evan McMullin in Utah. It was certainly late in the day — August 2016 — when McMullin, a former Capitol Hill staffer, launched his presidential campaign under the banner of 'Better for America'. McMullin's campaign grew out of the Never Trump movement made up of Republicans who refused to support or endorse Donald Trump. McMullin's support was concentrated in his native state of Utah where he attracted a significant amount of support from anti-Trump Republicans, especially among the large Mormon community. In the end, McMullin came in third, but with 21.5% of the vote, just 6 percentage points behind Clinton. He was also responsible for the collapse of the Republican vote in Utah from 73% in 2012 to just 45% in 2016.

Electoral College votes

There were two big Electoral College stories in 2016: the loser of the popular vote winning in the Electoral College, and the most defections from electors pledged to a living presidential candidate in US history. There have been years with a larger number of faithless electors, but only in the vice presidential contest, or when the presidential nominee to whom they were pledged died before the vote. It was also the first time since 1972 that a winning candidate had seen defections from his Electoral College votes. Table 5.4 gives us the details of the Electoral College defections in 2016 showing that Trump lost two electoral votes and Clinton five. The Trump electors in Texas voted one each for Governor John Kasich of Ohio and former Texas representative Ron Paul. Meanwhile in Hawaii, one Clinton elector voted for her primary opponent Senator Bernie Sanders of Vermont. But the most extraordinary goings-on occurred in Washington state where three Clinton electors voted for the former Republican Secretary of State Colin Powell, while one voted for a Native American elder and activist from South Dakota, Faith Spotted Eagle.

Table 5.4 Faithless presidential electors, 2016

State	Elector should have voted for	Actually voted for
Hawaii	Hillary Clinton	Bernie Sanders
Texas	Donald Trump	John Kasich
	Donald Trump	Ron Paul
Washington	Hillary Clinton	Colin Powell
	Hillary Clinton	Colin Powell
	Hillary Clinton	Colin Powell
	Hillary Clinton	Faith Spotted Eagle

There were also electoral votes going astray in the balloting for vice president. The elector in Hawaii who voted for Sanders for president voted for Senator Elizabeth Warren of Massachusetts for vice president instead of Tim Kaine. In Texas, the elector who voted for Kasich for president cast his vice presidential ballot for Republican primary candidate Carly Fiorina. Meanwhile, in Washington state, there was one vote each for vice president for Democratic senators Elizabeth Warren and Maria Cantwell, plus a vote for Republican Senator Susan Collins and the former Green Party vice presidential candidate Winona LaDuke.

Indeed, there could have been even more defections. Three other Democratic electors tried to vote for someone other than Hillary Clinton — one for Sanders in both Minnesota and Maine, and one for Kasich in Colorado. But each elector either changed their vote to Clinton or, when they failed to do so, were replaced by alternates who voted in the conventional way.

The irony in all this was that back in 2012, then private citizen Donald Trump had tweeted, 'The Electoral College is a disaster for democracy'. But maybe that was just a bit of fake news?

Split districts

In an ever more polarised America, there is evidence that there has been a significant decline in split-ticket voting — voting for candidates of different parties for different offices at the same election. Back in the 1970s and 1980s, it certainly was not unusual for voters to split their tickets — to vote, for example for the Democratic candidate for president but a Republican for the Senate, or the Republican candidate for president but a Democrat for the House. This led to a large number of what we call split districts — congressional districts which voted in the same election for a candidate of one party in the presidential election but a candidate of the other party in the House election. Figure 5.1 shows how the number of such districts has declined over the past four decades. One can see from this that back in the 1980s, there were at times getting on for 200 split districts representing some 45% of the total number. But by 2016, there were just 35 — or just 8% of the total.

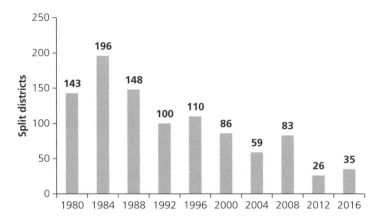

Figure 5.1 Split districts: 1980–2016

Of the 35 split districts in 2016, 23 of them were districts that voted for Democrat Hillary Clinton but a Republican House member, while the remaining 12 were districts that voted for Republican Donald Trump but a Democrat House member. Thus in the current House of Representatives there are 23 members we might describe as 'Clinton Republicans' and 12 members who we might call 'Trump Democrats'. Tables 5.5 and 5.6 show the split districts for each party in which the presidential candidate won by more than 10 percentage points.

Over half of the split districts were districts in which the presidential vote was close – either Clinton or Trump won by less than 5 percentage points. But 15 of them (43%) were districts in which either Clinton or Trump won by more than 5 percentage points, and eight of them were districts in which the presidential candidate won by more than 10 percentage points. In Minnesota's 7th district, Trump beat Clinton by over 30 percentage points, yet the same district re-elected Democrat Collin Peterson by 53% to 47%. But Peterson is one of the most conservative Democrats in the House. He voted against Obamacare in 2010, and has been endorsed by both the National Right to Life Committee and the National Rifle Association.

Table 5.5 Selected 'Trump Democrat' split districts

Congressional district	Presidential vote margin (%)	House vote margin (%)
Minnesota 7	Trump (R) +30.8	Collin Peterson (D) +5.1
Minnesota 8	Trump (R) +15.6	Rick Nolan (D) +0.6
Minnesota 1	Trump (R) +14.9	Tim Walz (D) +0.8
Pennsylvania 17	Trump (R) +10.1	Matt Cartwright (D) +7.6

Table 5.6 Selected 'Clinton Republican' split districts

Congressional district	Presidential vote margin (%)	House vote margin (%)
Florida 27	Clinton (D) +19.6	Ileana Ros-Lehtinen (R) +9.8
Florida 26	Clinton (D) +16.3	Carlos Curbelo (R) +11.7
California 21	Clinton (D) +15.5	David Valadao (R) +14.4
Virginia 10	Clinton (D) +10	Barbara Comstock +5.8

In Florida's Miami-based 27th district, Clinton beat Trump by just shy of 20 percentage points, yet the district also re-elected Republican Ileana Ros-Lehtinen. But Ms Ros-Lehtinen has a mainly liberal voting record in the House, becoming in July 2012 the first House Republican to support same-sex marriage. Nearly one-third (7) of all Clinton Republicans come from California, with Florida, Texas and Pennsylvania accounting for another seven. Most of the Trump Democrat districts are in the Northeast or the Midwest, while most of the Clinton Republican districts are in the Sun Belt, one of the few regions where Clinton improved on Obama's 2012 performance.

As a point of interest, it would be worth following the voting records of the Trump Democrats listed in Table 5.5 to see whether they show any particular trend to voting with Republicans given Trump's popularity in their districts. Similarly, do the Clinton Republicans in Table 5.6 show any particular trend to voting with the Democrats given the 2016 presidential vote in their district?

Senate races

Another piece of evidence of the increase in straight-ticket voting was seen in the Senate races in 2016. As recently as 1988, over half the Senate races were won by the party that lost that state in the presidential race. But in 2016, for the first time ever, all the Senate races were won by the party that won the presidential race in that state. Put another way, there are no Trump Democrats or Clinton Republicans in the Senate. That is a stunning turnaround in less than 30 years and shows the profound change that increased partisanship and polarisation has had on American elections during that period.

What is more, there was a close relationship between the Republican share of major-party votes for president and senator in 2016, particularly in the tightest contests. In Colorado, Nevada, New Hampshire, North Carolina, Pennsylvania and Wisconsin, the difference between the Republican presidential and the Senate vote share was no more than 1 percentage point (see Table 5.7). Thus Trump's unexpected victories in Wisconsin and Pennsylvania almost certainly helped Republicans retain control of the Senate, as did his victory in North Carolina, and provided more evidence of increased straight-ticket voting in American elections.

Table 5.7 Vote for Republican presidential and Senate candidates in selected swing states

State	Vote for Trump (%)	Vote for Republican Senate candidate (%)
Colorado	44	45
Nevada	45	45
New Hampshire	47	48
North Carolina	51	51
Pennsylvania	49	49
Wisconsin	48	49

Questions

1 What do the data in Table 5.1 tell us about the popular vote in the 2016 presidential election?
2 What problem for the Republicans does Table 5.2 highlight? What reason is suggested for the Republicans' difficulties?
3 Assess the importance of the role of third-party candidates in the 2016 presidential election.
4 To what extent did 'faithless electors' play a role in the 2016 presidential election?
5 Explain the terms 'Trump Democrats' and 'Clinton Republicans'.
6 What evidence is given for the rise of straight-ticket voting?

Chapter 6

The 2018 midterm congressional elections

On 6 November 2018, elections will be held for the whole of the House of Representatives and one-third of the Senate – those senators last elected in 2012. Races will also be held for the state governors in 36 states. Because these elections fall midway through the president's 4-year term, they are referred to as 'midterm elections'. But just before we get to these elections, we need to say something about the special Senate election in Alabama on 12 December 2017.

Alabama's special Senate election

When Republican senator Jeff Sessions of Alabama was confirmed as US attorney general in February 2017, he had to resign his Senate seat. The state governor of Alabama then nominated Luther Strange to fill the seat until a special election at the end of the year. But in September, Strange lost the Republican primary to the former chief justice of the Alabama Supreme Court, Roy Moore, despite being backed both by President Trump and the Republican Party establishment. Moore sits well to the right of the Republican mainstream and was supported by Republican voters frustrated by what they see as the 'politics-as-usual' of the party establishment in Washington.

But Moore was dogged throughout the general election campaign by accusations of sexual impropriety with young girls. He simply labelled his accusers as liars. After some initial reluctance, Moore received the backing of both President Trump and the Republican National Committee. But all to no avail. Moore lost to his Democratic challenger by 50% to 48% – the first time a Democrat had won a Senate race in Alabama since 1992. So what are the likely consequences of this embarrassing defeat? First, it was a significant slap in the face for President Trump. His candidate lost in a state that he had won by 28 percentage points just the year before. Second, it was a much-needed boost to the Democrats. They will feel that if they can win a such a deep red state as Alabama, they can win anywhere – though there were extenuating circumstances here. Third, it makes Trump's Republican majority in the Senate even more precarious, thus making legislative victories even more difficult to accomplish. Fourth, it might make conservative challenges to incumbent Republican candidates less likely in 2018. But finally, it just makes the upcoming midterm elections far more interesting and potentially significant.

Exit poll data from Alabama showed that Democrat Doug Jones was pushed over the winning line by the near-unanimous support of black voters, and by young voters. While white voters — who made up 66% of voters — split 68–30 for Moore, black voters (29% of voters) went for Jones by 96–4. Voters aged 18–44 (45% of voters) backed Jones 61–38, while the majority of voters aged 45 and over supported Moore.

Senate elections

So after the Alabama election, the Republicans enjoy party control of the Senate with just 51 seats, the Democrats have 47 seats and two independents both of whom usually vote with the Democrats make the party balance 51–49 in the Republicans' favour. As a result they control the chamber's leadership positions including that of majority leader (Mitch McConnell) and hold all the standing committee chairs. This is highly significant for the President especially in the areas of confirmation of appointments and investigation where party-line votes are common. Were the Democrats to win control of the Senate in these midterm elections, that would make life potentially much more problematic for President Trump during the next 2 years. He might find it much more difficult to win confirmation of more controversial appointments — especially of any to the Supreme Court — and might also find the committees more feisty in their investigation of him and his team.

On the face of it, the Democrats would seem to have quite a good chance of winning control of the Senate. They would need to make an overall gain of just two seats. (One gain would not be sufficient, as Vice President Pence would be able to break the tie in the Republicans' favour.) Furthermore, it is quite usual for the president's party to lose seats in the midterm elections.

But one other fact makes the Democrats' chances much less favourable — and that is that of the 33 seats up for re-election in 2018, only 8 of them are currently held by the Republicans. Twenty-three of them are already Democrat seats, and two are held by the independents Angus King of Maine and Bernie Sanders of Vermont. So winning two out of just eight while not losing any of their own 25 seats is something of a tall order. Furthermore, of the eight states held by the Republicans going into the 2018 Senate elections, seven of them are states won by Donald Trump in 2016. Only Dean Heller in Nevada is defending a Republican seat in a Clinton state. Indeed, Heller must be regarded as the most vulnerable Republican incumbent, especially as he won with only 46% of the vote in 2012 when the seat was last contested. But by contrast, 10 of the 23 Democrats are defending their seats in states that Republican Donald Trump won in 2016 and as Table 6.1 shows, some of those states were ones in which Trump won easily against Democrat Hillary Clinton. Based on the data in that table, Democrats in Indiana, Montana, North Dakota and Ohio would seem vulnerable to a strong Republican candidate.

Table 6.1 States in which incumbent Democrat senators are running in states won by Trump in 2016

State	Trump vote 2016 (%)	Clinton vote 2016 (%)	Democrat Senate vote 2012 (%)
Florida	49	48	55
Indiana	57	38	50
Michigan	48	47	58
Missouri	57	38	55
Montana	56	36	49
North Dakota	64	28	51
Ohio	52	43	50
Pennsylvania	49	48	54
West Virginia	69	26	61
Wisconsin	48	47	52

Another variable that will affect these races is how many incumbents decide to retire. Rates of re-election for incumbents are high in Senate races – over 80% in eight of the last nine election cycles, and exceeding 90% in three of them. Open seats – those in which no incumbent is running – tend to be easier for the 'out' party to win. The first senators to announce they would not be running for re-election were Republicans Bob Corker of Tennessee and Jeff Flake of Arizona.

But there is more potentially bad news for the Republicans and that is the factor we mentioned earlier – the trend for the president's party to lose seats in the Senate in midterm elections. Over the past six midterm election cycles – from 1994 to 2014 – the president's party has on average lost between 4 and 5 seats in the Senate. But the cycles vary hugely as Figure 6.1 shows. In 1998, President Clinton's Democrats actually managed to make an overall gain of 2 seats in the Senate, while in 2014, the Democrats made a net loss of 9 seats during the presidency of Democrat Barack Obama.

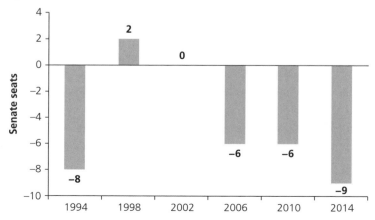

Figure 6.1 Number of Senate seats lost by the president's party in midterm elections, 1994–2014

Figure 6.2 shows that there is a high correlation between the president's approval rating and the performance of his party in the midterm elections. The only two midterm elections in the last six in which the president's party did not lose seats in the Senate saw the president with approval ratings above 60% — Clinton in 1998 and Bush in 2002. But those midterms in which the president's party suffered heavy losses coincided with presidential approval ratings below 50%. So history would tell us that one of the most important determinants of the outcome of these elections will be President Trump's approval ratings by Election Day. Given the way things stand as I write, the Republicans may well begin to feel somewhat pessimistic.

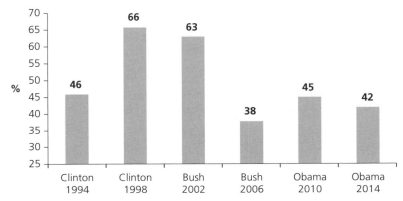

Figure 6.2 President's approval rating (%) at midterm elections, 1994–2014

House elections

All 435 House seats will be up for re-election in these midterm elections. At the time of writing the Republicans hold 241 seats to 194 for the Democrats, giving the Republicans a 47-seat majority. That means that the Democrats would need to make an overall gain of 24 seats in order to win party control of the House. So what's the record for the president's party in midterm elections in the House? Here we need to differentiate between those midterm elections that occur 2 years into a president's first term of office — like the 2018 midterms — and those that occur 2 years into his second term. Losses for the president's party in the House tend to be higher in the second midterms than in the first.

The average number of House seats lost by the president's party in the six first-term midterm elections between 1982 and 2010 was 29. But as Figure 6.3 shows, each cycle varies enormously between a gain of 5 seats for George W. Bush's Republicans in 2002 to a loss of 63 seats for Barack Obama's Democrats in 2010. As in the Senate, there is a correlation between the president's approval rating and losses for his party in the House in the midterm elections. When the president's approval rating was over 50% (see Figure 6.4), his party performed quite well in the midterm House elections, but when his approval fell below 50%, his party lost on average between 40 and 50 seats. So the question on our minds as election year dawns is, 'How would the Republicans do in the midterms were President Trump's approval ratings to be near or even below 40% in November?'

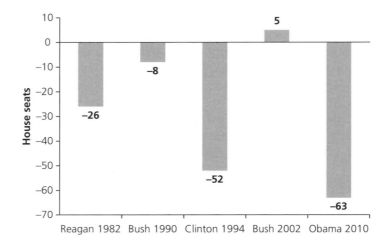

Figure 6.3 Number of House seats lost by the president's party in midterm elections during the first term, 1982–2010

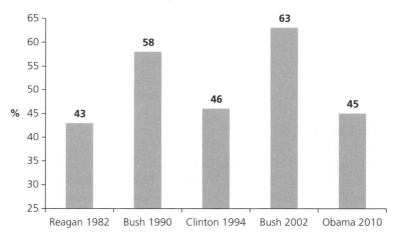

Figure 6.4 President's approval rating (%) at first-term midterm elections, 1982–2010

But we need to strike a note of caution for the Democrats. During the last decade or so, we have seen a significant decline in competitive districts – districts in which the margin of victory is less than 10%. As Figure 6.5 shows, the number of competitive House districts declined for six straight elections from 1994 to 2004, and although it peaked again in 2010 as the Republicans narrowly won a number of formerly Democratic seats, the number has declined in each of the last three election cycles. But what Figure 6.5 also shows very clearly is that in the 2018 midterm elections there will be only 31 competitive House races. Seventeen of those 31 competitive districts are being defended by the Democrats, leaving only 14 Republican-held seats in which the incumbent won in 2016 by less than 10 percentage points. Table 6.2 shows those 14 potentially vulnerable Republican House members in 2018. It also shows that only the top five in the table are super-marginal. That does not leave a lot of potential for the Democrats unless the economy implodes or Trump's approval rating continues at rock bottom – and that is still the great unknown about 2018.

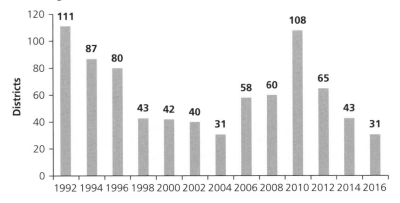

Figure 6.5 Competitive districts, 1992–2016

Table 6.2 House Republican incumbents in competitive districts

Republican incumbent	District	Margin of victory in 2016 (percentage points)
Darrell Issa	California 49	0.6
Don Bacon	Nebraska 2	1.2
Will Hurd	Texas 23	1.3
John Kline	Minnesota 2	1.8
Jeff Denham	California 10	3.4
Claudia Tenney	New York 22	5.5
Barbara Comstock	Virginia 10	5.8
Steve Knight	California 25	6.2
Rod Blum	Iowa 1	7.6
Mike Coffman	Colorado 6	8.3
Richard Hanna	New York 19	8.5
Brian Fitzpatrick	Pennsylvania 8	8.8
Bruce Poliquin	Maine 2	9.6
Ileana Ros-Lehtinen	Florida 27	9.8

So if the Democrats cannot rely on just flipping marginal Republican districts, they will need to look to other strategies to get their 24-seat gain. Possibly the most important, therefore, will be finding strong, well-financed challengers in seats where numerically the Republican incumbent looks quite safe. That was the strategy by which the Democrats took back control of the House of Representatives in 2006. Early signs are promising. Professor Larry Sabato, the elections guru at the University of Virginia, reported as early as August 2017 that there were even at that early stage 209 Democratic House challengers who had raised at least $5,000

or more, well up on previous cycles. What Democrats will therefore be hoping for is a field of strong, well-financed, viable challengers in seats currently held by Republicans that are not exactly competitive but which would be winnable with, as it were, a good following wind. In recent election cycles, the Democrats have made something of a habit of coming up short of even their quite modest expectations of gains in the House. They will be hoping that 2018 tells a different story.

Questions

1 What was the significance of the special Senate election in Alabama in December 2017?
2 What is the current party balance in the Senate?
3 Using the information and data given here, what do you think are the chances of the Democrats gaining control of the Senate in 2018? Give your reasons.
4 What factors are most likely to determine the outcome?
5 What is the current party balance in the House of Representatives?
6 Using the information and data given here, what do you think are the chances of the Democrats gaining control of the House in 2018? Give your reasons.
7 What factors are most likely to determine the outcome?

Chapter 7

Where is the Democratic Party going?

Down, down, down

The short answer to the question posed at the head of this chapter is that the Democratic Party is going down. Its support in almost every area of elective politics — federal, state and local, as well as legislative and executive — has declined precipitously since the early years of the Obama presidency just 8 years ago.

At the start of 2010, the Democrats of course controlled the presidency, having won 53% of the popular vote in 2008. Now in 2018, they are out of office as far as the White House is concerned, although their candidate Hillary Clinton did get more votes in 2016 than her Republican rival. Yet she still won only 48% of the popular vote. And in the Electoral College, the Democrats fell from 365 votes in 2008 to just 227 in 2016 — that means they lost more than one-third of their Electoral College votes over 8 years. And in the 2016 presidential election, they lost in Iowa for the first time since 2000, they lost in both Michigan and Pennsylvania for the first time since 1988, and they lost in Wisconsin for the first time since Ronald Reagan's 49-state re-election victory in 1984. The one bright piece of news for the Democrats, however, is that they have won the popular vote in six of the last seven presidential elections. It is just that they won in the Electoral College on only four of those occasions.

Eight years ago, the Democrats also controlled both houses of Congress. In the Senate they held 51 seats which, along with two independents, gave them an effective 6-seat majority over the Republicans. In the House, they held 258 seats to the Republicans' 177 seats, giving the Democrats a very sizeable majority of 81 seats. Now in 2018, they control neither chamber, with only 46 seats in the Senate — plus two independents — and just 194 seats in the House. In 8 years, they have lost 5 seats in the Senate and 64 in the House.

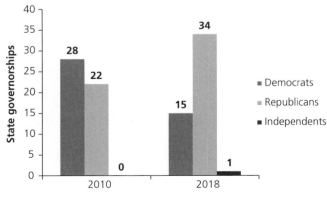

Figure 7.1 Party control of state governorships, 2010 and 2018 compared

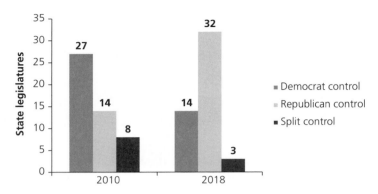

Figure 7.2 Party control of state legislatures, 2010 and 2018 compared

Eight years ago, the Democrats were the dominant party in state government, both in the executive and legislative branches. They controlled 28 of the state governors' mansions as well as controlling both houses of the state legislature in 27 states (see Figures 7.1 and 7.2). Indeed, in 16 states they controlled the governorship and both houses of the legislature (Figure 7.3). And 8 years ago, 55% of all state legislators were Democrats. Since then, they have lost 13 governorships – holding just 15 to the Republicans' 34 – and control of 13 state legislatures. Nearly 1,000 state legislative seats have been lost to the Republicans and today just 41% of all state legislators are Democrats (see Figure 7.4).

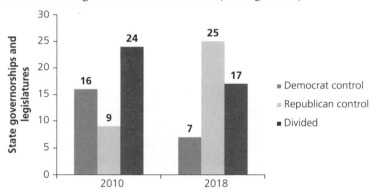

Figure 7.3 Party control of state governorships and legislatures, 2010 and 2018 compared

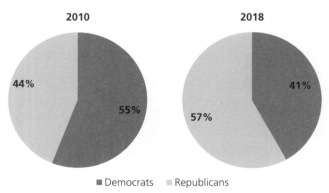

Figure 7.4 Party balance of state legislators, 2010 and 2018 compared

US Government & Politics

Down and divided

Not only has the party's hold on federal and state government been seriously eroded over the past 8 years, but the defeat of Hillary Clinton in the 2016 presidential election has left the Democratic Party without a unifying leader. Added to that, the fact that the party experienced a bitter campaign in the presidential primaries between Clinton and Vermont Senator Bernie Sanders left the party deeply divided after the election. As far as the party's national leadership is concerned, the Clinton wing of the party is certainly in control with Chuck Schumer as their leader in the Senate and Nancy Pelosi in the House. But this leadership team certainly does not have that 'new car smell'. Schumer is 67 and Pelosi 77 — and both are Capitol Hill veterans. Pelosi has been in the House for three decades while Schumer arrived in Congress the year Ronald Reagan moved into the White House — in 1981!

The Clinton wing of the party is also in control of the party's national headquarters — at the Democratic National Committee (DNC) situated just three blocks southwest of the Capitol in Washington, DC. The election of Trump further exacerbated the Democrats' internal divisions as the supporters of Bernie Sanders claimed that their candidate could have won the election, while Clinton supporters dismissed such claims as unfounded and ridiculous. This jostling for power between the supporters of Clinton and Sanders came quickly to the boil when a new chair of the DNC had to be chosen. And for the first time since 1985 there was a contest rather than a coronation with only one declared candidate. Ultimately, it came down to a choice between Tom Perez and Keith Ellison. Perez, formerly Obama's secretary of labor, was the establishment — Clinton wing — candidate. Minnesota Congressman Keith Ellison, the first Muslim elected to Congress, was supported by the 'Sandernistas'. In a close contest, Perez won by 235 votes to 200 with Perez then appointing Ellison as deputy chair.

The Clinton versus Sanders divide was evident once again in June 2017 when 30-year-old Democrat political newcomer Jon Ossoff lost a special election in Georgia's 6th congressional district to conservative Republican Karen Handel by less than 4 percentage points. Despite the fact that Georgia's 6th district has not elected a Democrat for 40 years, and that for 20 years (1979–99) it was represented by then Republican House Speaker Newt Gingrich, many more left-of-centre Democrats blamed the defeat on what they saw as the toxicity of Nancy Pelosi. The Democrats' civil war doesn't look like ending any time soon.

The Democrats' white working-class problem

Interviewed on CNN just a week after the Democrats' humiliating loss to Donald Trump in November 2016, Bernie Sanders made the following observations:

> I think there needs to be a profound change in the way the Democratic Party does business. I come from the white working class, and I am deeply humiliated that the Democratic Party cannot talk to where I come from.

So why does the Democratic Party continue to struggle so badly to appeal to working-class whites? In his post-election analysis, Nate Cohn writing in *The New York Times* had this to say:

> Trump spoke to their aspirations and fears more directly than any Republican candidate in decades. White Americans without a college degree voted decisively to reject the more diverse, educated and cosmopolitan Democratic Party of the 21st century in the onetime heartlands of 20th century liberal populism – the Upper and Lower Midwest.

Hillary Clinton had every reason to think that the Obama coalition – non-whites, young voters, single women and college-educated whites – would deliver her victory too. After all, the Republicans showed no obvious signs of trying to woo any of these demographic groups. The post-election analysis seemed to agree that Clinton's mistake was to fail to connect with the economic anxieties of working-class white voters precisely because she was over-confident that they would not go anywhere else. Furthermore, she would be criticised for failing to emphasise her economic message, spending much of her time merely attacking Trump for being Trump. For example, three-quarters of Clinton's television advertisements were about 'character' while just 9% were about jobs or the economy. This did not play well in the Rust Belt states nor in the Midwest.

Added to this, Clinton's Democrats in 2016 also failed to address the nationalist mood of the white working class. This nationalism had both economic and social as well as basic patriotic strands to it. Economic nationalism was about the perception of jobs being outsourced to foreign countries as well as jobs being given to foreign workers, and also American manufacturing facing unfair competition from foreign imports. Socially, working-class nationalism resented the Democrats' emphasis on multiculturalism and so-called 'gender equality'. The white working-class man felt Democrats at best ignored – and at worse sneered at – his belief in the values of old-fashioned, predominantly white communities made up of married folk one of whom was a man and the other a woman. Patriotically, working-class nationalism was all about 'making America great again' and that wasn't a tune the Democrats were singing.

Likely positives for Democrats in 2018…

As we saw in Chapter 6, the 2018 midterm elections offer both opportunities and challenges to the Democrats. The opportunities may be more in the state elections for governors and state legislatures; the challenges may be more in the congressional elections.

On the plus side for the Democrats, we have already seen in Chapter 6 that the president's party usually loses seats in the midterms. The Democrats might hope to make further gains on the back of Trump's record-breaking unpopularity by capitalising on public resentment of the President in particular and his administration in general. Furthermore, were the Republicans to come up short on genuine legislative achievements despite having controlled the presidency and both houses of Congress for the previous 2 years, that might make races more winnable for Democrats. Democratic strategist Brad Bannon commented: 'The general mood may grow more favourable for Democrats as we get further into a Trump administration.' It's also true that having been out of power in Washington for 2 years, Democratic candidates will more realistically be able to portray themselves as the 'agents of change' in 2018 than they could in 2016.

...and likely negatives

The Democrats will also face formidable challenges in 2018 — on top of those mentioned in the previous chapter. The central challenge is whether they can hold together the diverse and somewhat fragile coalition of voters that propelled Barack Obama to the presidency in 2008 and 2012 while at the same time making significant inroads with the white working-class voters who helped to elect Donald Trump in 2016. Figure 7.5 shows eight demographic groups in which the Democrats' support haemorrhaged badly between 2008 and 2016. Specifically, can the Democrats begin to win back such traditional Democrat voters as white, low-income and less-educated, middle-aged male voters? For it was in these groups that the Democrats' support dropped by between 6 and 12 percentage points in just 8 years. And can they win back the 18–29-year-old voters whose level of support for the Democrats fell from 66% in 2008 to just 55% in 2016?

The answer to those questions may depend on how effectively the Democrats manage to oppose the Trump agenda and whether or not the party can deliver a compelling and cohesive message about what it stands for. Merely being anti-Trump will not be enough.

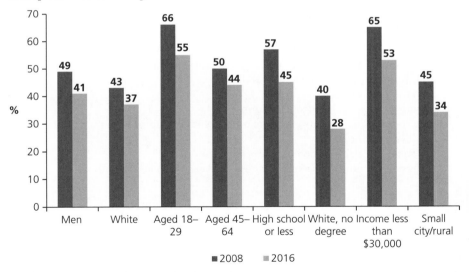

Figure 7.5 Democratic Party support among selected demographic groups, 2008 and 2016 compared

A Better Deal?

The small town of Berryville sits in the northwest corner of Virginia in the idyllic Shenandoah Valley. It is quintessential small-town America with a population of around 4,300 — up from under 3,000 just two decades ago. Arriving from

Washington, DC — 60 miles to the southeast — one is greeted by manicured lawns and independently run shops, evidence of a regular farmers' market and local vineyards, as well as a liberal scattering of impressively large churches. The population is 85% white with just 7% of inhabitants below the poverty line. In 2016, Clarke County, in which Berryville lies, went for Trump over Clinton by 20 percentage points — 57 to 37. In 2008, Obama lost to Romney by just 5 points. If the Democrats are to make a comeback in 2018 and 2020, they need to win back a lot of voters in the likes of Berryville.

In late July 2017, under a blazing summer sun, the Democratic Party's congressional leadership headed up State Route 7 to Berryville to launch their new policy agenda for 2018. The slogan — with apologies to Franklin Roosevelt (FDR) — was 'A Better Deal — Better Jobs, Better Wages, Better Future'. At a rally at Rose Hill Park just off Main Street, Senator Chuck Schumer proclaimed to a modest crowd of some 150 people:

> Democrats have too often hesitated from directly and unflinchingly taking on misguided policies that got us here. Too many Americans don't know what we stand for. Not after today. When you lose elections in 2014 and 2016 as we did, you don't flinch, you don't blink. You look in the mirror and ask: what did we do wrong?

So what was Schumer's answer?

> The number one thing we did wrong is not present a strong, bold economic agenda to working Americans so that their hope for the future might return again.

Box 7.1 **'A Better Deal'**

Some of the early-announced policy proposals included:

- $1 trillion infrastructure plan
- minimum wage increase to $15 an hour
- paid family sick leave
- lowering prescription drug charges
- new regulations to limit business mergers in an attempt to crack down on corporate monopolies
- expansion of apprenticeship programmes
- tax credit for employers to train new workers to fill vacancies

---

Not everyone was immediately impressed. One news outlet described the policy proposal as 'anodyne' and 'a kinder, gentler populism' while others mocked the attempt to mimic FDR's New Deal. Meanwhile, wags on Twitter couldn't resist the similarity of the policy's strapline to that of the popular pizza restaurant and takeaway franchise Papa John's Pizza which proclaims 'Better Ingredients, Better Pizza'. Indeed, some Republican supporters in Berryville held up pizza boxes bearing the slogan: 'Better Skills, Better Jobs, Better Wages — Still Pelosi!'

But what the Democrats are up against is the widespread perception revealed in a *Washington Post–ABC News* poll published around the same time as the Better Deal launch that while 37% of Americans believe the Democratic Party 'stands for something', 52% believe it 'just stands against Trump' (see Figure 7.6). And even among Democrats, more than a quarter believed that their party was little more than anti-Trump. Figure 7.6 also shows that the Democrats have got their work cut out to persuade Republicans, independents, and white, less-educated, middle-aged men that they actually stand for something substantial at all.

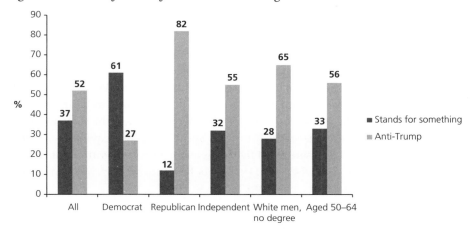

Figure 7.6 'Do you think the Democratic Party currently stands for something or just stands against Trump?'

Source: Washington Post–ABC News poll, 10–13 July 2017

And what about 2020?

Here again, it would be easy for the Democrats to fall into the trap of over-optimism — believing that President Trump will inevitably be a one-term president. For a start, incumbent presidents — presuming if we may that Trump runs for a second term — are extremely difficult to defeat. As Table 7.1 shows, of the ten incumbent presidents to run for re-election since Dwight Eisenhower in 1956, only three have been defeated, and one of those — Gerald Ford in 1976 — had never been elected as president. Indeed, Jimmy Carter (1980) and George H. W. Bush (1992) are the only two elected incumbents to be defeated in over 80 years.

Table 7.1 Incumbent presidents running for re-election, 1956–2012

Year	Incumbent president running for re-election	Result
1956	Dwight Eisenhower (R)	Won
1964	Lyndon Johnson (D)	Won
1972	Richard Nixon (R)	Won
1976	† Gerald Ford (R)	Lost
1980	Jimmy Carter (D)	Lost
1984	Ronald Reagan (R)	Won
1992	George H. W. Bush (R)	Lost
1996	Bill Clinton (D)	Won
2004	George W. Bush (R)	Won
2012	Barack Obama	Won

† Appointed president 1974

Second, it won't necessarily be easy for the Democrats to win back voters that supported Obama in 2008 and 2012 but who left the party to vote for Trump in 2016. As Brandon Finnigan, the director of the non-partisan election site Decision Desk HQ commented recently, in some parts of the country 'Democrat voters stampeded to Trump – they didn't just move to Trump, they ran to him.' Finnigan added: 'It would be a massive event for them to come stampeding back in one cycle.'

And third, it is possible that as one looks at the presidential election map that some states may be slipping away from the Democrats. We have already seen this happen in previous election cycles in which states such as West Virginia and Missouri where Democrats used to have a reasonable chance of winning have become more Republican. So, for example, the Democrats won in West Virginia in 1988, 1992 and 1996 – respectively by 5, 13 and 15 percentage points – but the Republicans have won the state in all five subsequent elections, winning the state 68% to 26% in 2016. Likewise, the Democrats have not won in Missouri since 1996, losing by 18 percentage points to Trump in 2016.

And it's possible that states such as Iowa, Minnesota and Wisconsin might also be trending Republican. Figure 7.7 shows how the Democrat share of the vote in these three states has fallen between 1988 and 2016 – two comparable elections which were both won by the Republicans in a two-horse race. In Iowa in 1988, Democrat Michael Dukakis won with 55% of the vote beating Vice President Bush by 11 points. But in 2016, Hillary Clinton lost the state to Trump by 9 points, 51–42. As Brad Finnigan commented: 'This doesn't mean a Democrat won't win these states ever again, or that the Republicans have a lock on them. But they've red-shifted.' He also suggested that similar trends were discernible in both Pennsylvania and Michigan.

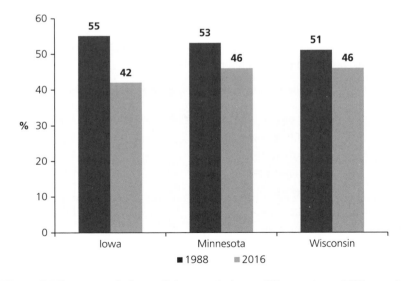

Figure 7.7 Democrats' share of the vote in Iowa, Minnesota and Wisconsin, 1988 and 2016 compared

Two health warnings

In closing, two health warnings. Warning number one: be very sceptical of articles that use the term 'the Democratic Party base' to refer to the supporters of Bernie Sanders pushing for economic populism and more progressive, left-wing policies. That presumption flies in the face of two facts. One, that Hillary Clinton tied with Bernie Sanders among Democratic primary voters who described themselves as 'very liberal'. Second, that it was Hillary Clinton who won the majority of Democratic voters in the Democratic primaries while Sanders picked up much of his support from independent and non-aligned voters. True, the Democratic Party seems to be moving leftwards — mostly under the influence of Sanders and his surrogates — but 'the Democratic Party base' is still Clinton country.

Shortly after Democrat Lyndon Johnson overwhelmed Republican Barry Goldwater in the 1964 presidential election, the then doyen of political scientists Nelson Polsby declared that America's two-party system had ended and that from that point on the country would see a 'one-and-a-half party system' with the Republicans serving the inevitable role of being the nation's 'half party'. Yet a mere 4 years later, Republican Richard Nixon was walking into the Oval Office, to be re-elected another 4 years later in a 49-state landslide. Indeed, the Republicans would win five of the next six presidential elections. The moral of the story is that forecasting the electoral health of political parties can be a hazardous business. True, the Democrats face significant challenges in the upcoming electoral cycles. But then, the Republicans' electoral ship is not exactly sailing on untroubled waters. So health warning number two is: don't write off the Democrats.

Questions

1 What do the data in Figures 7.1 to 7.4 tell us about the Democratic Party during the past 8 years?
2 How did the Clinton–Sanders divide in the party continue in evidence after the 2016 elections?
3 Why did the Democrats have a problem with white working-class voters in 2016?
4 What positives and negatives does the Democratic Party face going into the 2018 midterm elections?
5 Briefly outline what the Democrats are hoping to achieve by the launch of 'The Better Deal'.
6 What challenges are likely to face the Democrats in the 2020 presidential race?
7 Why should we be cautious about writing off the Democrats as a political and electoral force?

Chapter 8

Is the Trump cabinet merely a mirror image of the president?

What you need to know

- The president's cabinet is not mentioned in the Constitution.
- By tradition, the cabinet consists of the heads of the executive departments which now number 15.
- The president, at his discretion, awards cabinet rank to other administration officials.
- The cabinet meets as a group only occasionally and intermittently at the president's request.
- Cabinet members therefore exist for most of the time as individuals whose principle function is to run their departments and lobby Congress for the legislation they want to see passed and the money they need for their department.

A reflection of the boss

Presidential cabinets tend to be a reflection of the boss in a number of ways. In modern times, the youngest ever cabinet was appointed by President Kennedy — the youngest ever elected president. Ronald Reagan, on the other hand, who was 69 when he became president, appointed what was at that time (1981) the oldest ever cabinet. Kennedy's cabinet also included a number of people from the Northeast and New England — Kennedy was from Massachusetts. Reagan's cabinet included a number of people from California — Reagan's home state — and the Midwest where Reagan had spent some of his early life. In the end, it can often come down to simply who the incoming president knows. For, unlike the UK prime minister, incoming American presidents have no shadow cabinet upon which to draw.

Recruiting elected politicians

An incoming president, like Donald Trump in 2017, often wants to recruit people to his cabinet with some experience of elective politics. After all, one of the main functions of cabinet members — especially those who head up the 15 executive departments — is to work with members of Congress, both to secure the department's budget allocation and to gain passage of legislation in which the department is interested. So it helps to know people, and to know the way the process works.

But recruiting members of Congress into the cabinet is hard work. Because of the strict separation of personnel between the executive and legislative branches of the federal government, accepting a cabinet post means resigning from Congress.

Given the lack of job security in the cabinet and the high levels of re-election in Congress, this makes a cabinet post very unattractive to a serving member of Congress. Of the 152 people who have served in the president's cabinet as head of an executive department since 1981, just 12 had served in the Senate and 18 only in the House, meaning that fewer than one in five had any experience in Congress. Of those 30, just 13 were serving in Congress when they were recruited – including Senator Jeff Sessions (Justice) and Representatives Ryan Zinke (Interior) and Tom Price (Health and Human Services) in the original Trump cabinet.

During this same period – 1981 through 2017 – 17 former state governors have served in the cabinet, including Sonny Perdue (Agriculture) and Rick Perry (Energy) in the original Trump cabinet. Governors bring both links with state governments and also executive experience. Add in four city mayors, one state legislator and one local official, and elected politicians accounted for just under 35% of all cabinet members during the past 36 years. Those departments that have attracted the most elected politicians in this period are Health and Human Services (7) and Agriculture (6), with Defense, Interior, Transportation and Energy each attracting five.

Gender

It was President Gerald Ford who was the first president in modern times to appoint a woman to his cabinet as head of an executive department. (Franklin Roosevelt had appointed Frances Perkins as secretary of labor back in 1933.) It was 1975 and Ford needed someone to head the Department of House and Urban Development (HUD) to replace James Lynn whom Ford had just appointed as director of the Office of Management and Budget. At the time Carla Hills was working at the Department of Justice when she received a phone call from the White House. When I interviewed Ms Hills a few years later she told me:

> I knew the President was looking for someone at HUD. He called me by phone and asked me to go over to the White House where I met the President. When he offered me the HUD job, I was very surprised as I had no background in urban affairs – nor in the housing business. I told the President, 'I believe you'll have some political flak in not nominating someone with a background in the policy area concerned.' He said he didn't believe so. What he needed, he said, was a good administrator and I had a reputation as such.

But once Carla Hills had broken the glass ceiling, there was hardly a stampede of women into the president's cabinet. In the period from Reagan to Trump, only 17% of heads of the executive departments have been women. And as Table 8.1 shows, the increases witnessed during the presidencies of Bill Clinton, George W. Bush and Barack Obama have been reversed during the initial cabinet appointments of Donald Trump. Trump's is the most male-dominated cabinet for nearly four decades.

Table 8.1 Number of women appointed by presidency, Reagan to Trump

President	Women in original cabinet	Women as replacement appointments	Total
Ronald Reagan	0	3	3
George H. W. Bush	1	2	3
Bill Clinton	3	2	5
George W. Bush	3	3	6
Barack Obama	4	4	8
Donald Trump	2	0	2

Race

It was much the same when it came to race. It was President Lyndon Johnson who made the breakthrough there when, in 1966, he appointed African-American Robert Weaver to head the newly created Department of Housing and Urban Development. Five years earlier, Kennedy had appointed Weaver as head of the Housing and Home Finance Agency (HHFA) – the body that was transformed into HUD by Johnson in 1966. But when I interviewed Weaver in 1981, he explained that even his appointment to head the HHFA in 1961 had been highly controversial, mainly because he was black:

> There was a great deal of opposition to my 1961 appointment. Mine and [the President's brother] Robert F. Kennedy's [as Attorney General] were the only two really given a going-over by the Senate in confirmation hearings. I had met JFK maybe three times before he nominated me in 1961, but I doubt he would have remembered me from Adam's cat! I had been vice president of the NAACP and knew that he did not tend to vote with us on civil rights bills. So I was a bit apprehensive. But I was quite favourably impressed and gradually got to like him. Then I got to know Johnson from serving with him on the Equal Opportunities Commission.

And as with women, it took some time for Johnson's ground-breaking appointment to catch on. Having partly desegregated the cabinet, Johnson handed over to Nixon in 1969 who appointed all white members throughout his presidency. It was another 9 years after Weaver's appointment before another black was appointed to the cabinet – Ford's appointment of William Colman at Transportation. Like Ford, the next three presidents seemed to appoint a token black member – Carter appointing Patricia Roberts Harris first to HUD and then to Health and Human Services (HHS), Reagan appointing Samuel Pierce at HUD, and the first Bush appointing Louis Sullivan at HHS. It is also worth noting that, as with women, blacks were being appointed to the lower-level, client-based departments such as housing, health and transportation. The departments of state, defense, the treasury and justice were still white male bastions.

Table 8.2 Number of blacks appointed by presidency, Reagan to Trump

President	Blacks in original cabinet	Blacks as replacement appointments	Total
Ronald Reagan	1	0	1
George H. W. Bush	1	0	1
Bill Clinton	4	3	7
George W. Bush	2	2	4
Barack Obama	1	4	5
Donald Trump	1	0	1

Clinton did appoint four blacks to his first cabinet which was — and remains — a record (see Table 8.2), but they were still being appointed to lower-tier departments (see Table 8.3). It wasn't until George W. Bush's administration in 2001 that African-Americans were appointed to top-tier departments. Indeed, during his 8 years in office, Bush was served by two African-American secretaries of state — Colin Powell and Condoleezza Rice, respectively the first black man and the first black woman to hold the post.

Trump's appointment of just one black to his initial cabinet — and that to a lower-tier department — turns the clock back to the 1980s. Trump's only African-American head of department is Ben Carson at HUD, the department that is in danger of becoming the token black's posting. After Andrew Puzder withdrew from his nomination as secretary of labor, Trump later nominated Alex Acosta, a 48-year-old Hispanic academic from Florida. But in terms of both gender and race, Trump's cabinet looks much more like the latter decades of the last century than the second decade of this century.

Table 8.3 Blacks appointed to Clinton's cabinet

Name	Department
Original appointments	
Mike Espy	Agriculture
Ron Brown	Commerce
Hazel O'Leary	Energy
Jesse Brown	Veterans Affairs
Replacement appointments	
Alexis Herman	Labor
Rodney Slater	Transportation
Togo West	Veterans Affairs

The only other Trump cabinet member from an ethnic minority other than Carson is a retread from the Bush cabinet — Elaine Chao who is now at Transportation. But she also just happens to be the wife of Senate Republican leader Mitch McConnell. So one wonders whether Chao's Chinese heritage had much to do with her appointment. *The New York Times* wrote that 'taken as a whole, [the

cabinet] are striking for their uniformity'. But that's actually a quotation from 50 years ago and the incoming Nixon cabinet. But Trump seems to have taken a leaf out of the Nixon cabinet appointment book. It's just that it now looks half a century out of date.

Age

In 1961, John F. Kennedy famously remarked in his inaugural address that 'the torch has been passed to a new generation of Americans'. Donald Trump in 2017 made a good fist of passing it back again. While Kennedy appointed the youngest ever cabinet with an average age of just 47, Trump has appointed the oldest ever cabinet with an average age of 63. But then Kennedy came to office at the age of 43, while Trump was 70 — respectively the youngest and oldest elected presidents. Presidents tend to pick their contemporaries. As Table 8.4 shows, only one executive department head was under 55 on appointment and three were over 70, including Commerce Secretary Wilbur Ross at 79.

Table 8.4 Trump's initial cabinet by age

Age	Cabinet members
70+	Wilbur Ross (79), Jeff Sessions (70), Sonny Perdue (70)
65–69	John Kelly (67), James Mattis (66), Rick Perry (66), Ben Carson (65)
60–64	Rex Tillerson (64), Elaine Chao (63), Tom Price (62)
55–59	Betsy DeVos (59), David Shulkin (58), Ryan Zinke (55)
50–54	Steven Mnuchin (54)
45–49	Alex Acosta (48)

Figure 8.1 shows how much the average age of the cabinet has varied over the past half-century but that at 63, Trump's is significantly older than any of his immediate predecessors.

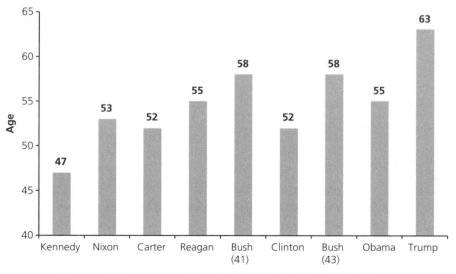

Figure 8.1 Average age of original cabinets: Kennedy to Trump

The cabinet as a mirror of Trump

As Henry C. Jackson wrote on the *Politico* website on Trump's fourth day in office: 'Trump's cabinet is older, whiter and richer than his predecessors' cabinets' ('Trump's cabinet by the numbers', 24 January 2017). And those are not the only ways in which the Trump cabinet looks like a mirror image of the President himself. Their wealth makes them look like Trump. Commerce Secretary Wilbur Ross is reportedly worth $2.5 billion – and that's more than the combined personal wealth of Obama's and Bush's first cabinet which would have been around $315 million. And then there's Trump's Education Secretary Betsy DeVos whose family is worth more than $5 billion. The wealthiest cabinet member in the first Obama cabinet was Hillary Clinton at just $31 million.

Then there's something else many of his cabinet share with Trump – their lack of any governmental experience. Six of Trump's heads of department have no government experience including Secretary of State Rex Tillerson and Secretary of the Treasury Steven Mnuchin. Furthermore, many of these folk drawn from outside government come, like Trump, from the world of business and corporate finance. Rex Tillerson is the former CEO of ExxonMobil, the oil giant. Steven Mnuchin comes from Goldman Sachs.

Trump is clearly attracted politically to older, white, wealthy men with a background in business and finance. In other words, the Trump cabinet does look remarkably like their septuagenarian business tycoon of a boss. The message was clear: less well-off, young women from ethnic minorities need not apply.

Senate confirmation

All of Trump's cabinet picks were the subject of a recorded vote on the floor of the Senate. None was agreed by voice vote as is often the case with non-controversial appointments. As Table 8.5 (p. 58) shows, Veterans Affairs Secretary David Shulkin received a unanimous vote having previously served as number two in the same department for the last 18 months of the Obama administration. A further four of Trump's cabinet received only token opposition ranging between one and eleven 'no' votes. But at the other end of the scale, six nominees received more than 40 'no' votes including Betsy DeVos who had to rely on the tie-breaking vote of Vice President Mike Pence to be confirmed in a vote of 51–50. The closeness of the vote resulted from all 48 Democrats being joined by two Republicans – Lisa Murkowski and Susan Collins – in voting 'no'.

Senate Republican leader Mitch McConnell had to schedule the vote on Betsy DeVos before the one on Senator Jeff Sessions to become Attorney General because the Republicans needed Sessions's 'yes' vote to get DeVos confirmed. Had Sessions already been confirmed as Attorney General he would have had to resign from the Senate thereby making him unable to vote. The DeVos vote would then have been lost 49–50. When Vice President Pence voted to confirm DeVos, this was the first time a vice president had cast a tie-breaking vote since Vice President Dick Cheney's vote on 13 March 2008. Joe Biden held the office for 8 years under President Obama but was never called upon to cast a tie-breaking vote.

Table 8.5 Confirmation votes for Trump's initial cabinet (in order of Senate vote)

Post	Nominee	Senate vote
Secretary of Veterans Affairs	David Shulkin	100–0
Secretary of Defense	James Mattis	98–1
Secretary of Transportation	Elaine Chao	93–6
Secretary of Homeland Security	John Kelly	88–11
Secretary of Agriculture	Sonny Perdue	87–11
Secretary of Commerce	Wilbur Ross	72–27
Secretary of the Interior	Ryan Zinke	68–31
Secretary of Energy	Rick Perry	62–37
Secretary of Labor	Alex Acosta	60–38
Secretary of Housing and Urban Development	Ben Carson	58–41
Secretary of State	Rex Tillerson	56–43
Secretary of the Treasury	Steven Mnuchin	53–47
Attorney General (Department of Justice)	Jeff Sessions	52–47
Secretary of Health and Human Services	Tom Price	52–47
Secretary of Education	Betsy DeVos	51–50

Other cabinet members

By tradition, the president's cabinet is made up of the heads of the executive departments, currently numbering 15. But the president may also use his discretion to award cabinet rank to other administration officials. Indeed certain discretionary posts have now been awarded cabinet rank by so many successive presidents that they are almost regarded as traditional members – the vice president, the US trade representative, the US ambassador to the United Nations and the director of the Office of Management and Budget to name but four. President Trump awarded cabinet rank to nine members of his administration (see Table 8.6).

Table 8.6 Discretionary members of the Trump Cabinet

Post	Office holder
Vice President of the United States	Mike Pence
White House Chief of Staff	† John Kelly
US Trade Representative	Robert Lighthizer
Director of National Intelligence	Dan Coats
US Ambassador to the United Nations	Nikki Haley
Director of the Office of Management and Budget	Mick Mulvaney
Director of the Central Intelligence Agency	Mike Pompeo
Administrator of the Environmental Protection Agency	Scott Pruitt
Administrator of the Small Business Administration	Linda McMahon

† Replaced Reince Priebus, July 2017

Replacement appointments

It is highly unusual for a president to make changes in his cabinet personnel during his first year in office. Going back as far as President Kennedy in 1961, the only president to make a change in cabinet personnel during their first year was Bill Clinton who announced the resignation of his first secretary of defense, Les Aspin, on 15 December 1993 — after just under 11 months in office. But Aspin served through to February 1994 thereby completing just over a year in post. Barack Obama managed to keep his initial cabinet together for over 2 years. The first change came in April 2011 when his secretary of defense, Robert Gates, announced his departure. But by this time, Obama had been in office for over 2 years and 3 months. Furthermore, Gates was a holdover appointment from the George W. Bush administration, so Gates had held the Pentagon post since December 2006, over 2 years before Obama arrived in the Oval Office.

So for President Trump to announce his first cabinet change after just 190 days was certainly extraordinary. This occurred on 28 July 2016, when Trump appointed Secretary of Homeland Security John Kelly as the new White House chief of staff to replace Reince Priebus who had been fired. This left a critically important executive department leaderless just 6 months into the Trump presidency. And then in September, Health and Human Services Secretary Tom Price resigned after it was revealed that he had taken expensive charter and military flights at taxpayers' expense. He might have also been paying the price for failing to get the repeal and replace of Obamacare through Congress (see Chapter 1). Earlier in the year, Trump had publicly joked that if the repeal and replace legislation failed in Congress, Price would be fired. So just 8 months into his presidency, the President had already lost two of his cabinet.

Cabinet meetings

The frequency with which presidents hold cabinet meetings varies hugely from president to president. Obama tended to average around 6 per year, slightly less than George W. Bush. Clinton used the cabinet very sparingly, while Reagan held frequent meetings. The functions of cabinet meetings can also differ from one administration to another. One president, such as George W. Bush, might use them mainly for discussion of big-ticket, cross-departmental issues. Another president, such as Ronald Reagan, might use them to check up on where major legislation had got to in its passage through Congress, while another — Jimmy Carter — used them to find out what was going on in each executive department.

On 12 June, almost 5 months into his presidency, President Trump tweeted, 'Finally held our first full cabinet meeting today. With this great team, we can restore prosperity and bring real change to [Washington] D.C.' This first full cabinet meeting certainly made headlines, but for all the wrong reasons. After some prepared introductory remarks — interspersed with some of Trump's trademark ad-libbing — the President suggested that they went round the table introducing themselves. This does draw attention to a serious point, that the president's cabinet is often a cabinet of strangers. There will be many unfamiliar

faces around the table — both to other cabinet members and even maybe to the president himself. Indeed, Trump didn't get off to the best of starts, seeming not to recognise his own vice president. 'I'm going to start with our vice president,' said Trump swivelling his head around the table — and even behind him — trying to locate Mike Pence, before suddenly noticing that Pence was sat in the vice president's designated seat at the cabinet table, directly opposite the president! 'Oh, there he is,' said Trump jovially to a chorus of muffled titters around the room. 'We'll start with Mike, then we'll just go around, your name, your position.' Trump was beginning to look and sound like a teacher talking to new students on their first day of school.

But being in the presence of the president of the United States of America tends to turn grown-up, sensible human beings into fawning lapdogs. Shown live on the Fox News channel, the resulting minutes were excruciating as each person around the table competed to make the most fulsome compliments to their beloved boss. Vice President Pence got the ball rolling when rather than merely saying, 'I'm Mike Pence and I'm the vice president', opted instead for:

> The greatest privilege of my life is to serve as vice president to a president who is keeping his word to the American people, assembling a team that's bringing real change, real prosperity and real strength back to our nation.

That set the bar pretty high, but one has to say that cabinet colleagues rose to the occasion (see Box 8.1) talking of the 'honour', 'privilege' and even 'blessing' of serving in the president's cabinet. The whole occasion was variously described in the media as 'surprisingly creepy' (MSNBC), 'bizarre' (ABC News), 'awkward' (CNBC), 'weird' (CNN) and 'obsequious' (The *Guardian*).

Box 8.1	Extracts from cabinet members' remarks to the President at the start of Trump's 12 June 2017 cabinet meeting

- **Steven Mnuchin (Treasury):** 'It was a great honour travelling with you around the country and an even greater honour to be here serving in your Cabinet.'
- **Mike Pompeo (CIA):** 'Mr President, it's an honour to serve as your CIA director.'
- **Jeff Sessions (Justice):** 'It's so great to be here.'
- **Sonny Perdue (Agriculture):** 'I want to congratulate you, Mr President, on the men and women you've placed around this table. These are all great team members and we're on your team.'
- **Tom Price (Health):** 'Mr President, what an incredible honour it is to lead the Department of Health and Human Services. I can't thank you enough for the privileges you've given me and the leadership that you've shown.'
- **Reince Priebus (Chief of Staff):** 'Let me thank you, Mr President, for the opportunity and the blessing that you've given us to serve your agenda.'

Because of the need for cabinet members to get to know each other — and the president — and because of the need for the president to instil his agenda into his team, presidents tend to hold more cabinet meetings in the opening months of their presidency than at any other time during their administration. President Obama held five cabinet meetings between April and November of 2009 — his first year in office — with no longer than a 2-month gap between meetings. But come his third year in office, there was a 6-month gap between a meeting in February and the next in August. By his second term, Obama was down to about two or three meetings a year.

So one should not read too much into the frequency of Trump's early cabinet meetings. The first five came respectively on 13 March (though not all members had been confirmed), 12 June, 31 July, 9 September, 16 October and 1 November, which was roughly in line with what occurred in the Obama administration. Trump, like a number of his predecessors, will doubtless see cabinet meetings as a useful public relations exercise, pushing the image of collegial decision-making and a team fully focused on 'making America great again'.

Questions

1 Why is it difficult for incoming presidents to attract serving members of Congress into their cabinet? How successful was Trump in this respect?
2 What other experience of elective politics did Trump's cabinet members bring?
3 To what extent did Trump appoint a balanced cabinet in terms of gender and race?
4 What do Table 8.4 and Figure 8.1 tell us about the age of Trump's cabinet?
5 In what ways does this new cabinet provide a mirror image of President Trump?
6 How easily were Trump's initial cabinet nominees confirmed?
7 What was remarkable about Trump's cabinet meeting on 12 June 2017?
8 Why do presidents tend to hold more cabinet meetings early in their administrations?

Chapter 9

The Trump presidency: an early assessment

Just after Franklin D. Roosevelt had been elected to the presidency in November 1932, Walter Lipmann — then the nation's foremost political commentator — wrote of Roosevelt that he was 'a pleasant man, without any qualifications for the office', which only goes to show that making early assessments of presidents is a tricky business! And what is also proving tricky during the early months of the Trump era — and will doubtless continue to be the case for as long as it lasts — is discerning the fact from the fiction. But as I write this — 9 months into the Trump administration — there are, I think, six important trends which one can discern.

Six important trends of the Trump presidency's first year

1 Trump is trying to govern as the outsider he promised to be.
2 Trump has little interest in legislation.
3 Trump's White House has been largely dysfunctional.
4 The Trump administration is dogged by scandal and apparent dishonesty.
5 Trump's approval ratings have been at historically low levels.
6 Donald Trump is a deeply polarising figure.

Trump is trying to govern as the outsider he promised to be

In 2016, Donald Trump conducted a successful hostile takeover of the Republican Party. Of the 17 candidates who entered the Republican primaries in 2016, 14 of them were professional politicians — part of the Republican Party establishment. Trump was one of the three that wasn't. And he made it clear he had no time for 'business as usual' in Washington — describing the city as a 'swamp' that he would 'drain'.

Even after he won the party's nomination, he made little or no attempt to reach out to congressional Republicans, let alone anyone from the other side. Leading politicians were publicly denigrated by Trump with nicknames that sounded like those used by a bully in a school playground — Little Marco (Rubio), Lyin' Ted (Cruz), Low Energy Jeb (Bush), and of course Crooked Hillary (Clinton). Now in the White House, Trump continues in the same vein extending the name-calling to leaders of foreign nations, most notably referring to North Korea's leader Kim Jong-un as 'Rocket Man' during his speech to the United Nations General Assembly in New York. (Trump later 'improved' on this, calling Kim 'Little Rocket Man' at a rally in Alabama a few days later.)

The trouble is that although one can run successfully as an outsider in a nomination race and even in an election, governing requires a different approach. Once you arrive in the White House, you are — like it or not — part of the Washington establishment, and you need to build bridges to members of Congress of both parties. Donald Trump is certainly not the first president to struggle to build working relationships with members of Congress, but he must be the first to openly denigrate and criticise members of Congress from his own party on a regular basis. In his first 9 months in office, Trump openly criticised at least eight Republican senators including the majority leader (Mitch McConnell), the chairman of the foreign relations committee (Bob Corker) and the former presidential candidate and war hero John McCain. When your party has a majority of only 2 seats in the chamber, that really makes no sense at all. What is more, both Corker and Jeff Flake of Arizona — two senators whom Trump has repeatedly and publicly mocked — had announced before the year's end that they would not seek re-election in 2018 thereby possibly making their seats more vulnerable and further threatening the Republican's narrow majority in the Senate.

Trump has little interest in legislation

Because Trump still tries to act as an outsider, he has little interest in discovering the details of the legislative initiatives he often talks and tweets about. From those closely involved in the major legislative initiatives thus far during the Trump presidency, we learn that Trump has little grasp of any detail of the legislation he proposes or even of the legislative process itself. In a press briefing in the Oval Office in late-February alongside his then Secretary of Health and Human Services Tom Price, this is how Trump talked about his new healthcare plan — to repeal and replace Obamacare:

> We have a plan that's going to be **fantastic**. I think it's going to be **something special**. The new plan will be a **great** plan, and I think that people are going to **like it a lot**. We look forward to providing healthcare that is **extraordinary**, better than any other country anywhere in the world — and we can do that.

So there you have it. Trump's healthcare plan is 'fantastic', 'something special', 'great' and 'extraordinary'. And just a week before the first failed vote on the plan in Congress, Trump was tweeting:

> Despite what you hear in the press, healthcare is **coming along great**. We are talking to many groups and it will end in a **beautiful** picture!

In an interview with *Forbes* magazine later in the year, the President talked excitedly about 'an economic-development bill which I think will be **fantastic**'. But these are not the kind of descriptions that are going to sway votes on the floor of the House or the Senate. As a consequence, Trump moved towards the first anniversary of his inauguration with unified party control of the White House and Congress but having failed to sign a single piece of significant legislation. In his first 9 months, President Obama signed a wide-ranging economic stimulus package, along with legislation to give relief for the hard-pressed mortgage and car-manufacturing industries, plus a significant hate crime bill. Those all ranked as significant legislative accomplishments. For Trump, as November of his first year dawned, there was nothing.

Trump's White House has been largely dysfunctional

When Republican Senator Bob Corker of Tennessee was on the receiving end of a Twitter storm from the President one October morning, the Senator tweeted back: 'It's a shame the White House has become an adult day care centre. Someone obviously missed their shift this morning.' Ouch! If that's what the President's supposed supporters are saying, you can imagine what his opponents are thinking.

One of the first photographs to come out of the working White House of President Trump showed a scene of apparent business and purpose. The President was on the phone, seated at his Oval Office desk the surface of which was stacked with files and papers. Standing or sitting around the desk were five men who were either engrossed in the papers they were holding or participating in whispered conversation. The impression given was of a president at work surrounded by his key aides and advisers. Sitting at the desk were Vice President Mike Pence and National Security Adviser Mike Flynn. Standing behind them were Chief of Staff Reince Priebus, Chief Strategist Steve Bannon and Press Secretary Sean Spicer. But just 7 months later, all bar the vice president were gone (see Table 9.1). One is reminded of Lady Bracknell's famous put-down of Mr Worthing in Oscar Wilde's *The Importance of being Earnest* when Worthing tells her that he has lost both his parents: 'To lose one parent may be regarded as a misfortune; to lose both looks like carelessness.' Well, for the President to lose four of his top staffers looked like gross carelessness and fuelled the belief that the Trump White House is largely dysfunctional. To use Mr Trump's favoured business comparisons, it's not successful firms that fire their top management, but failing ones.

Table 9.1 Changes in key White House staff members: February–August 2017

Post	Original holder	Resigned/sacked	Replacement
National Security Adviser	Mike Flynn	13 February	H. R. McMaster
Press Secretary	Sean Spicer	21 July	Sarah Sanders
Chief of Staff	Reince Priebus	28 July	John Kelly
Chief Strategist	Steve Bannon	18 August	*No replacement*

Box 9.1 **Extracts from *The New York Times* interview with Senator Bob Corker (R–Tennessee), chairman of the Senate Foreign Relations Committee, 8 October 2017**

The President concerns me. I know for a fact that every single day at the White House it's a situation of trying to contain him. It's a daily exercise at the White House to keep him in the middle of the road. The tweets, especially as they relate to foreign policy issues, I know have been very damaging to us. I do wish that would stop.

Look, except for a few people, the vast majority of [Republican senators] understand what we're dealing with here. There will be some — if you write that — I'm sure will say, 'no, no, no I don't believe that,' but of course they understand the volatility that we are dealing with and the tremendous amount

> of work that it takes from people around [Trump] to keep him in the middle of the road. No question.
>
> Sometimes I feel like he's on a reality show of some kind, you know, when he's talking about these big foreign policy issues. And, you know, he doesn't realise that we could be heading towards World War III with the kinds of comments he's making.
>
> And it's like it's an act to him that bothers me...but I don't think he understands. When I watch him on television and sometimes it very much feels to me that he thinks as president he's on a reality television show. And I don't think he understands that the messages he sends out, especially when you take into account they're being received in other languages around the world, what that does. I know he's hurt us as it relates to negotiations that were underway by tweeting things out.
>
> I don't think he fully appreciates that when the president of the United States speaks and says the things he does, the impact that it has around the world. It's just totally impulsive. It's like he's doing 'The Apprentice'. He's just putting on an act, and it's worrying. You have people out there working hard to solve problems, and those kind of statements set us back. They just do.

During the first vital 6 months of his presidency, Trump's White House seemed to be in a constant state of turmoil and leaked like a sieve. Insiders reported that things in the West Wing were 'chaotic' and that 'the paper flow [was] erratic'. Priebus was unable to control the flow of either people or paper into the Oval Office while a long-time friend of the President, Christopher Ruddy, commented in public that the chief of staff was 'in way over his head'.

So when Priebus was replaced by General John Kelly, many hailed this as the pivotal moment of the Trump presidency after which order and crisp management would be brought to a White House desperately in need of both. There's no doubt that Kelly did bring order to the West Wing in the months that followed, but the self-inflicted wounds kept coming. Even if Kelly was able to control who and what entered the Oval Office, not even he could control Trump's Twitter feed. And there lies one of the main problems of the Trump administration. Kelly and others could spend hours, days, weeks or months carefully lining up policy proposals, smoothing over the President's missteps and misspeaks, trying to make the unworkable work, but all their efforts can be blown away in just a couple of minutes and 140 characters.

Table 9.2 shows among other things the extent of White House dysfunction that was on full view during the last 10 days of July 2017. It also illustrates in the October entries the President's habit of replying to criticism with aggression no matter who is involved — whether it is a member of Congress or a grieving widow. Trump has certainly lived up to his lifelong mantra of 'never apologise'. But that, too, becomes costly.

One thing we learnt during the days of President Richard Nixon: that the way the White House works reflects the way the president works. The Nixon White

House was secretive and paranoid because Nixon was secretive and paranoid. The same rule applies today: the Trump White House is largely dysfunctional because Donald Trump is largely dysfunctional.

Table 9.2 Trump presidency timeline: January–October 2017

Date	Event
27 January	Trump signs 'Muslim travel ban'
30 January	Trump fires Acting Attorney General Sally Yates
3 February	Federal judge suspends Trump's 'Muslim travel ban'
13 February	National Security Adviser Michael Flynn resigns
14 February	Trump requests FBI Director Comey to shut down Flynn investigation
16 February	Trump's approval rating falls below 50% for the first time
20 March	FBI Director Comey reveals the bureau is investigating possible Russian influence in the 2016 election and possible links between Russia and the Trump campaign
22 March	Trump complains to Director of National Intelligence Dan Coats and CIA Director Mike Pompeo about the FBI's investigation of the 2016 election
23 March	The first major vote on legislation to repeal and replace Obamacare is postponed
4 April	Trump's approval rating falls below 40% for first time
7 April	Senate confirms Neil Gorsuch as an Associate Justice of the Supreme Court
4 May	House votes to repeal and replace Obamacare (217–213)
9 May	Trump fires FBI Director James Comey
10 May	Trump is alleged to have divulged classified intelligence information in a meeting with Russian diplomats in the Oval Office
17 May	Former FBI Director Robert Mueller appointed as Special Counsel to oversee the investigation into links between Russia and the 2016 election and related subjects
8 June	Healthcare reform legislation fails in the Senate
21 June	Anthony Scaramucci appointed as White House communications director White House Press Secretary Sean Spicer resigns All four votes in the Senate to repeal and replace Obamacare fail
28 June	Chief of Staff Reince Priebus is fired to be replaced by General John Kelly
31 June	Anthony Scaramucci is fired after just 10 days in post
8 August	Trump issues a statement that if North Korea continues to make threats 'they will be met with fire and fury like the world has never seen'
12 August	Demonstration by KKK, Neo-Nazis and White Supremacists in Charlottesville, VA, ends with one dead and 19 injured. Trump issues a statement condemning 'the egregious display of hatred, bigotry and violence on many sides'.

Date	Event
18 August	Chief Strategist Steve Bannon is fired
6 September	Trump cuts a deal with the Democrats to keep federal government funded and raise the nation's borrowing authority
14 September	Trump cuts a deal with the Democrats to support legislation to protect 'Dreamers' from deportation in exchange for a 'massive' increase in border security — but not with a wall
22 September	Graham–Cassidy bill to repeal and replace Obamacare falls in Senate without a vote
16 October	Representative Frederica Wilson (D-Florida) discloses to the press that in a phone call to the widow of a US soldier recently killed in Niger, President Trump had said in reference to her late husband that 'he knew what he had signed up for, but I guess it still hurt'.
18 October	President Trump claims that Representative Wilson's version of events is 'totally fabricated' and that he had 'proof' that this was so
19 October	Chief of Staff John Kelly accuses Representative Wilson of 'grandstanding' at an event in 2015 to dedicate an FBI building in Florida, calling her 'an empty barrel'
20 October	Video of the 2015 FBI dedication event surfaces showing that Kelly's claim was false
23 October	Myeshia Johnson, widow of the slain soldier Sgt La David Johnson, goes on ABC's *Good Morning America* and says how upset she was by the President's phone call because of his insensitive remark and that he had difficulty remembering her husband's name. President Trump immediately takes to Twitter denying Mrs Johnson's claims

The Trump administration is dogged by scandal and apparent dishonesty

Lest I should be accused of being overtly and unfairly critical of Mr Trump, I have chosen my words carefully here. Whatever one thought of the policy achievements of the Obama administration, it had the significant virtue of being pretty much a scandal-free zone for the entire 8 years of its life. Not only were the President and First Lady excellent role models in integrity and propriety, but both the West Wing and the cabinet were unsullied by any significant scandal. Given the media's penchant for attaching 'gate' to any political scandal — in memory of Watergate — that four-letter suffix remained pretty much unused between 2009 and the start of 2017. Indeed, with the odd notable exception, much the same could be said of the presidency of George W. Bush in the previous 8 years. Donald Trump's administration seems to be making up for lost time.

Even before he entered the White House there were allegations of scandal surrounding Trump's campaign, most notably of possible collaboration between members of the Trump campaign organisation — even possibly of the Trump family — and folk with ties to Vladimir Putin's government in Moscow who might have been attempting to swing the election in Trump's direction. Furthermore, there was the ongoing controversy of Trump's refusal to release his tax returns. Every

president back to and including Richard Nixon has released his tax returns for public scrutiny both before and after his election to office, as have their respective vice presidents. Every presidential candidate of both parties in 2016 released their tax returns – except for Donald Trump. What is more, Trump gives specious and misleading reasons for withholding this information. This clearly adds to an appearance of scandal. There were also serious allegations raised during the 2016 campaign about Mr Trump's mistreatment and sexual harassment of women.

Then there is the President's benefiting from his own business interests while in office. Government officials, visiting dignitaries and lobbyists have stayed in hotels and resorts bearing Trump's name. The Trump International Hotel in Washington, DC – opened in 2016 just five blocks from the White House – has become the place of choice to wine, dine and reside for those coming to the city to do business with the Trump administration. Trump's Mar-a-Lago club in Florida, where the President has spent many a weekend break, doubled its membership rates after Trump was elected. And in just the first 9 months in office, Trump had spent more than $30 million of taxpayers' money travelling to and from properties he owns. And although during that same period Trump spent only 8 days in Trump Tower in New York, the government has leased space in the building – at $130,000 per month – for a military office that supports the President when he is there.

There have also been numerous accusations that the President has attempted to influence government officials in ways that raise serious questions about propriety. Just a week into office, it is alleged that Trump invited the then Director of the FBI James Comey to a private, one-on-one dinner at the White House at which he requested a pledge of loyalty from the director and asked Comey whether he (Trump) was the subject of an FBI investigation. In mid-February in another private meeting with Comey at the White House, it is alleged that the President requested Comey to shut down an investigation into Trump's former national security adviser Mike Flynn. It is also alleged that in mid-March the President tried to enlist the help of Director of National Intelligence Dan Coats and CIA Director Mike Pompeo to persuade FBI Director Comey to pull back on his investigations into possible links between the Trump campaign and the Russian government. Some would see this as treading a very fine line on obstruction of justice. In May, Trump fired Director Comey and then allegedly boasted to a group of Russian diplomats in the Oval Office that this would take the heat off him regarding the Russia controversy. Trump even appeared to threaten Comey that he had tapes of their conversations in a failed attempt to stop Comey from giving his side of their one-on-one conversations. At the time of writing all these allegations – and they remain only that – were being investigated by the Special Counsel Robert Mueller (see Chapter 4). But all this certainly gives the Trump White House an appearance of impropriety.

Added to all this is the President's ingrained habit of exaggeration, false credit-claiming and – to call it what it is – downright lying. In an interview in late October of 2017, Republican Senator Bob Corker accused the President of 'constant non truth-telling, name calling and the debasement of our nation'. That's strong stuff coming from a fellow Republican.

At the root of all this seems to be Trump's overly developed sense of personal importance — that everything is about him. When a Category 5 hurricane hit Florida, he wanted everyone to know that his administration was getting 'great reviews' for the way it was handling the crisis. When a similar catastrophe hit Puerto Rico, Trump wanted us to know how difficult solving this crisis was for him, and that the fault for any poor response lay only with the political leaders on that ravaged island. When an American serviceman was killed on active service in Niger, Trump wanted everyone to know that in a phone call to the soldier's widow:

> I was extremely nice to her. I've never seen her, I've never met her, but she sounds a lovely lady. But I was extremely nice to her, I was extremely courteous, as I was to everyone else.

One cannot help but notice that the subject of each sentence is 'I'. So even in a story of deep human grief, Trump is compelled to make himself the centre of attention. Many of these Trump traits were undoubtedly what former President George W. Bush had in mind in a rare public speech he gave in late October 2017 (see Box 9.2).

Box 9.2	**Extracts from speech by President George W. Bush to an invited audience in New York City, 19 October 2017**

Bigotry seems emboldened. Our politics seems more vulnerable to conspiracy theories and outright fabrication.

We have seen our discourse degraded by casual cruelty. At times, it can seem like the forces pulling us apart are stronger than the forces binding us together. Argument turns too easily into animosity. Disagreement escalates into dehumanisation.

Bullying and prejudice in our public life sets a national tone, provides permission for cruelty and bigotry, and compromises the moral education of children. The only way to pass along civic virtues is to first live up to them.

On top of all this, various members of the Trump administration have themselves been involved in various matters of potentially unethical behaviour:
- Interior Secretary Ryan Zinke is under investigation for chartering a $12,000 flight from Las Vegas to Montana at taxpayers' expense
- Veterans Affairs Secretary David Shulkin charged taxpayers for a trip to Europe that included sightseeing in London and a visit to Wimbledon, plus a cruise on the River Thames for himself and his wife
- Treasury Secretary Steve Mnuchin allegedly used a taxpayer-funded military plane to travel to view the solar eclipse in August 2017
- Health and Human Services Secretary Tom Price resigned after admitting he had spent hundreds of thousands of taxpayers' dollars on hiring private jets
- Trump adviser Kellyanne Conway was reprimanded for promoting Ivanka Trump's fashion line on television

And if that were not enough, there is suspicion that the President's two elder sons and his son-in-law, Jared Kushner, are using their closeness to Trump to promote their various business interests.

Trump's approval ratings have been at historically low levels

Presidential approval is these days measured almost continuously by a host of polling organisations. 'Do you approve or disapprove of the job X is doing as president?' is the question posed. It is meant to be vague rather than measuring performance in any particular policy area. Presidents like to keep their percentage approval rating above 50% – that is more folk approving than disapproving. Table 9.3 shows the number of weeks that passed before a president's approval rating fell below 50% and below 40% for the first time. On this measure, George W. Bush scores highest, helped of course by the huge boost in his approval rating following the 9/11 attacks during his first year. Bush had been in office for 157 weeks before his approval rating fell below 50%, and for 244 weeks before he went below 40%. By contrast, Trump's approval (as measured by the Gallup Organisation) has never reached 50% – the highest was 45% in his first week – and fell below 40% after just 8 weeks in office.

Table 9.3 Number of weeks in office before approval rating fell below 50% and 40% (selected presidents)

President	Number of weeks in office before below 50%	Number of weeks in office before below 40%
George W. Bush	157	244
George H. W. Bush	152	161
Richard M. Nixon	109	231
Jimmy Carter	57	77
Barack Obama	42	*Never below 40%*
Ronald Reagan	41	52
Bill Clinton	16	20
Donald Trump	*Always below 50%*	8

Source: www.gallup.com

Another way of comparing Trump's approval rating with his near predecessors is to compare the average approval rating for the first three quarters of each presidency (see Figure 9.1). This shows that Trump's first quarter (first 3 months) average of just 41% was lower than any of the other presidents' averages for any of their first three quarters. This data shows starkly how historically low Trump's approval rating has been during the first 9 months of his presidency. Low presidential approval at this stage in an administration has usually meant three things:

- low levels of success in passing the president's policy programme through Congress
- losses for the president's party in midterm elections
- a one-term presidency

The first has certainly been the case up to now. We shall know about the second later in 2018. But unless Trump can shift these numbers significantly upwards, talk of a two-term Trump presidency might be somewhat premature.

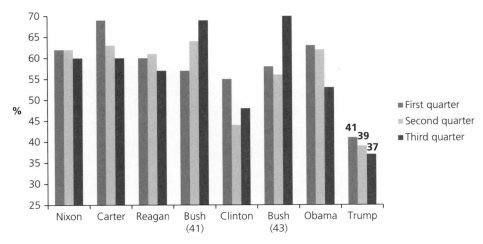

Figure 9.1 Average presidential approval ratings for first three quarters: Nixon to Trump

Source: www.gallup.com

Donald Trump is a deeply polarising figure

Finally, Table 9.4 shows that Trump has been the most politically divisive president in modern history. Although Trump has very similar levels of support from his own party as Obama, Bush, Clinton and Reagan did from theirs, his support from opposition party identifiers is way down on his recent predecessors — especially on the levels recorded by Bush, Clinton and Reagan during their 8 years in office. Hence the partisan gap — at 76 percentage points — is easily the highest since the data began to be available some seven decades ago. The polarising nature of Trump's policies and personality mean that in reality he is not president of the United States but merely president of the 'deep red' areas of America where his core supporters live. It is to them he speaks, acts, visits and tweets. It is an America made up mostly of deeply frustrated, resentful, white, middle-aged, lower middle-class and blue-collar Americans who live mainly in the small towns and rural areas of the South and the Midwest. And the future of Trump's presidency depends largely on how long he can sustain their unquestioning support. Time — as well as polls and election results — will tell.

Table 9.4 Partisan gap of presidential approval: selected presidents compared

President	Average % approval: own party	Average % approval: opposition party	Partisan gap in approval average
Donald Trump	84	8	76
Barack Obama	83	13	70
George W. Bush	84	23	61
Bill Clinton	82	27	55
Ronald Reagan	83	31	52
Richard Nixon	75	34	41
George H. W. Bush	82	44	38
Jimmy Carter	57	30	27

Questions

1 What problems has President Trump created in his relationship with Congress?

2 What is Trump's approach to the formulation of legislation and policy making?

3 Give some examples of the ways in which the Trump White House has been somewhat dysfunctional.

4 Why does the author think that General John Kelly will still face challenges as White House chief of staff?

5 What do we learn about President Trump from the remarks made by Senator Bob Corker (Box 9.1) and former president George W. Bush (Box 9.2)? How objective do you think these remarks are?

6 Give some examples of the scandals that have dogged the Trump administration thus far.

7 Give some examples of what the author calls 'Trump's overly developed sense of personal importance'.

8 What do the data in Table 9.3 and Figure 9.1 tell us about Trump's level of public approval during his first 9 months in office? Visit **www.gallup.com** and **www.realclearpolitics.com** to find out more up-to-date information on this.

9 What do the data in Table 9.4 tell us about Trump as a polarising figure? What do you think makes President Trump such a polarising figure?

Who's who in US politics 2018

The executive branch

President	Donald Trump
Vice President	Mike Pence

The cabinet

Secretary of State	Rex Tillerson
Secretary of Defense	James Mattis
Secretary of the Treasury	Steven Mnuchin
Attorney General (Justice Department)	Jeff Sessions
Secretary of Agriculture	Sonny Perdue
Secretary of the Interior	Ryan Zinke
Secretary of Commerce	Wilbur Ross
Secretary of Labor	Alex Acosta
Secretary of Health and Human Services	Alex Azar
Secretary of Education	Betsy DeVos
Secretary of Housing and Urban Development	Ben Carson
Secretary of Transportation	Elaine Chao
Secretary of Energy	Rick Perry
Secretary of Veterans Affairs	David Shulkin
Secretary of Homeland Security	Kirstjen Nielsen

Executive Office of the President personnel

White House Chief of Staff	General John Kelly
Counsellor to the President	Kellyanne Conway
Director of Office of Management and Budget	Mick Mulvaney
Chairman of Council of Economic Advisers	Kevin Hassett
Domestic Policy Council Director	Andrew Bremberg
National Security Adviser	H. R. McMaster
Director of Legislative Affairs	Marc Short
Director of National Trade Council	Peter Navarro
Press Secretary	Sarah Huckabee Sanders

Other executive branch personnel

Director of Central Intelligence Agency (CIA)	Mike Pompeo
Director of Federal Bureau of Investigation (FBI)	Christopher Wray
Chairman of the Joint Chiefs of Staff (JCS)	General Martin Dempsey

Legislative branch

Senate leadership

President Pro Tempore of the Senate   Orrin Hatch (R-Utah)
Senate Majority Leader   Mitch McConnell (R-Kentucky)
Senate Minority Leader   Charles Schumer (D-New York)
Senate Majority Whip   John Cornyn (R-Texas)
Senate Minority Whip   Richard Durbin (D-Illinois)

Senate standing committee chairmen

Agriculture, Nutrition and Forestry   Pat Roberts (Kansas)
Appropriations   Thad Cochran (Mississippi)
Armed Services   John McCain (Arizona)
Banking, Housing and Urban Affairs   Richard Shelby (Alabama)
Budget   Michael Enzi (Wyoming)
Commerce, Science and Transportation   John Thune (South Dakota)
Energy and Natural Resources   Lisa Murkowski (Alaska)
Environment and Public Works   Jim Inhofe (Oklahoma)
Finance   Orin Hatch (Utah)
Foreign Relations   Bob Corker (Tennessee)
Health, Education, Labor and Pensions   Lamar Alexander (Tennessee)
Homeland Security and Governmental Affairs   Ron Johnson (Wisconsin)
Judiciary   Charles Grassley (Iowa)
Rules and Administration   Roy Blunt (Missouri)
Small Business and Entrepreneurship   David Vitter (Louisiana)
Veterans Affairs   Johnny Isakson (Georgia)

House leadership

Speaker of the House of Representatives   Paul Ryan (R-Wisconsin)
House Majority Leader   Kevin McCarthy (R-California)
House Minority Leader   Nancy Pelosi (D-California)
House Majority Whip   Steve Scalise (R-Louisiana)
House Minority Whip   Steny Hoyer (D-Maryland)

House standing committee chairmen

Agriculture   Michael Conaway (Texas)
Appropriations   Harold Rogers (Kentucky)
Armed Services   Mac Thornberry (Texas)
Budget   Tom Price (Georgia)
Education and the Workforce   John Kline (Minnesota)
Energy and Commerce   Fred Upton (Michigan)
Financial Services   Jeb Hensarling (Texas)

Foreign Affairs	Edward Royce (California)
Homeland Security	Michael McCaul (Texas)
Judiciary	Bob Goodlatte (Virginia)
Natural Resources	Rob Bishop (Utah)
Oversight and Government Reform	Jason Chaffetz (Utah)
Rules	Pete Sessions (Texas)
Science, Space and Technology	Lamar Smith (Texas)
Small Business	Steve Chabot (Ohio)
Transportation and Infrastructure	Bill Shuster (Pennsylvania)
Veterans Affairs	Jeff Miller (Florida)
Ways and Means	Kevin Brady (Texas)

Judicial branch

		Appointed by	Year appointed
Chief Justice	John Roberts	George W. Bush	2005
Associate Justices	Anthony Kennedy	Ronald Reagan	1988
	Clarence Thomas	George H. W. Bush	1991
	Ruth Bader Ginsburg	Bill Clinton	1993
	Stephen Breyer	Bill Clinton	1994
	Samuel Alito	George W. Bush	2006
	Sonia Sotomayor	Barack Obama	2009
	Elena Kagan	Barack Obama	2010
	Neil Gorsuch	Donald Trump	2017